A CYCLING GUIDE
FROM
LANDS END TO
JOHN O'GROATS

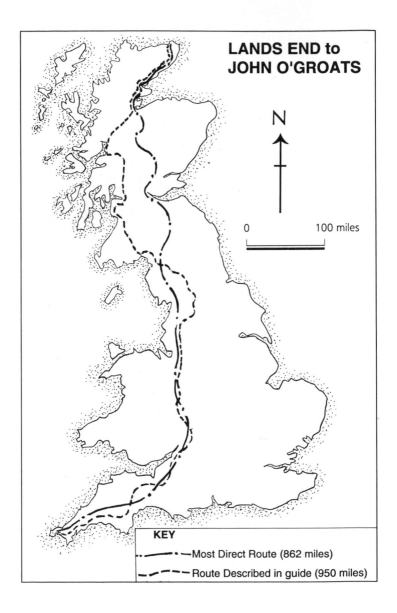

LANDS END to JOHN O'GROATS

N

0   100 miles

KEY

—·—·— Most Direct Route (862 miles)

— — — Route Described in guide (950 miles)

A CYCLING GUIDE
FROM
LANDS END TO
JOHN O'GROATS

by

Simon Brown

CICERONE PRESS
MILNTHORPE, CUMBRIA, UK

© Simon Brown 1995
ISBN 1 85284 188 5
A catalogue record for this book is available from the British Library

DEDICATION

To my wife, Tina

ACKNOWLEDGEMENTS
Sincere thanks are extended to all the cycling clubs and organisations that have contributed to the compilation of the guide and to the Regional Tourist Offices and County Councils for information concerning established cycle routes. Thanks to Ali Read and Tina Brown who accompanied me on the trip and to Andy Peckham and British Rail for providing the transport at either end. Thanks also to all the help and encouragement from people too numerous to mention along the route.

Front Cover: Easier ground as the route follows the picturesque shores of Loch Tulla before climbing to the plateau of Rannoch Moor and on to Glen Coe

CONTENTS

Introduction

Routes

ADVICE TO READERS

Readers are advised that whilst every effort is taken by the author to ensure the accuracy of this guidebook, changes can occur which may affect the contents. A book of this nature is more prone to change than a more general guide. It is advisable to check locally on transport, accommodation, shops, etc.

The publisher would welcome notes of any changes.

Photographs and sketches by the author

INTRODUCTION

The British Isles provides perhaps some of the best cycle touring country in Europe. The diversity of landscape and culture within this relatively small land mass is quite unique and cycling offers the ideal method to explore its many and varied facets. The cycle tourer is fortunate to be able to share the intimacy of the landscape with the hiker, but with an added mobility that allows many times the distance to be covered. Many local tours are open to the aspiring cycle tourist, exploring country lanes that weave a course through the historic past of rural Britain. Many local authorities are now actively promoting these routes in response to greater public demand and a whole new generation are discovering the joys of this relaxing pastime. Perhaps the ultimate cycle tour would be one that interlinks these unique areas and on a single trip explores the full spectrum of diversity of terrain found throughout the country: the wild open moorland of the south-west, the peaks of the central Pennine chain, the glaciated inheritance of Cumbria and the highlands of Scotland.

Such a tour certainly exists and is not beyond the capabilities of any reasonably fit person. It runs from Lands End in the south-west to John O'Groats in the north-east and has been the inspiration for many endurance records and pleasure trips alike. Everybody who has successfully completed the journey by whatever means has a story to tell and are proud to join the celebrated group of "End to Enders".

HISTORY

The bicycle has been in existence for the last 150 years. During this time it has served as both a practical means of transport and a focus for leisure travel. The initial concept of pedal travel came from Germany in 1817. The two-wheeled contraption took the market by storm. Ironically, the Hobbyhorse as it was affectionately known was never pedalled but merely scooted along by the rider's feet and it wasn't until around 1860 that pedals were introduced. The Boneshaker employed a direct drive to the front wheel which limited its flexibility for normal use, so consequently was only actively endorsed by enthusiasts. Man's insatiable lust for speed ensured that faster machines were developed. This was principally achieved by increasing the diameter of the front wheel, reaching its ultimate conclusion in the ludicrously styled Penny-farthing.

The modern cycle came with the invention of chain drive, gearing and the pneumatic tyre, offering a cheap and practical method of transport into the 20th century. It was during this period of boom that the cycle manufacturers were anxious to increase the sales of their cycles by demonstrating the effectiveness of their product. Cycling sports were eagerly contested and sponsorships for feats of endurance were offered.

Reports of rides approaching 1000 miles are documented before the turn of the century and one of the first successful rides from Lands End to John O'Groats took place in 1880. The Roads Record Association was formed in 1888 and the first official time recorded over the distance has been accepted as 65 days 16 hours 7 minutes ridden in 1885 on a Penny-farthing!

The simplicity and affordability of the cycle ensured its popularity in Britain up until the outbreak of the Second World War when the development of motorised transport diverted attention away from the humble bike.

Recent changes of social attitude and a greater environmental awareness has resulted in a rebirth of popularity for the cycle. There are now an estimated 15 million in use in Britain today and the proportion of adult/child owners has increased, which is encouraging. Cycling offers one of the most accessible sport or leisure activities; anybody can do it and there are many active clubs throughout the country to encourage those who are not so sure. Activities range from road racing, cycle touring and time trials to simple afternoon trips into the country with a group of friends. Off road riding has also increased in popularity with the recent introduction of the All Terrain Bike (ATB).

More and more people are discovering the freedom offered by two wheels. The 30,000 that take part in the annual 50-mile ride from London to Brighton is testimony to that. There are many tours available to the cycle tourist within the British Isles. Many people choose short day trips from a central base while others opt for longer trips around selected areas of interest. Whatever the facet of the sport, it is now universally accepted that cycling comes with considerable health benefits as well as simply being a great way to get about whether your bike is being used for daily commuting or round the world tours.

LANDS END TO JOHN O'GROATS

With the introduction of high technology cycle parts, dedicated training schedules and back-up facilities the time taken to complete the distance from Lands End to John O'Groats has been reduced to an unbelievable 1 day 21 hours completed in 1990 by A. Wilkinson. The immensity of this achievement can never be overestimated but it is not the purpose of this guide to infringe on the world of road racing.

Perhaps one of the greatest aspirations of any cyclist is simply to complete the tour from Lands End to John O'Groats. It remains today one of the great distance yardsticks of the British Isles. Many people have risen to the challenge and consequently the course has been completed on foot, backwards, on one wheel, two wheels and three wheels, on a bed and even a motorised barstool! Indeed the route is completed annually by many people. This does not detract from the achievement or the enjoyment of the trip. The exact course followed between these two extremes of the country also varies as much as the method of transport chosen and it would be presumptuous for this guide to suggest one route over all others. The route followed by the guide is not the shortest distance between the two points - that is being left to the road racers - but one that is achievable in a single two-week period whilst taking in as much of the scenic beauty of the country as possible. Above all the aim is to enjoy the trip whilst at the same time exploring parts of the country that are sometimes overlooked by the tourist. For this reason it is by no means definitive and individuals may wish to vary the itinerary to encompass their own particular areas of interest. Where obvious variations are possible these are mentioned in the text.

The route chosen for this guide begins at the tip of Cornwall and diverts almost immediately from the direct route to take in the scenery of the south coast before crossing the remote wilds of Dartmoor into Somerset. The route heads north to the Bristol Channel where it traces the Welsh border through the Midlands. The Cumbrian Cycle Way offers a connecting link between the Lakes and the Pennines and delivers the tourer in 7 days to the Scottish border. A course north-west through Dumfries and Galloway joins the Sustran cycle routes by the coast and continues across the Erskine Bridge to the banks of Loch Lomond. Classic Scottish highland scenery continues through Glen Coe and Fort William on the west coast before the banks of Loch Ness are followed to the east coast. A coastal route then continues north-east to reach John O'Groats.

The Guide

The route has been described in a south to north direction. Although this is psychologically "uphill all the way" it does take advantage of the prevailing south-westerly winds. The total distance covered is just under 950 miles and has been broken down into 14 daily rides averaging 68 miles per day. The maximum distance travelled in one day is 88.7 miles.

Each section begins with a summary of the day's route together with total distance covered and estimated cycling time. The time quoted does not allow for stops of any kind and assumes a steady pace on a laden bike.

Details are then provided of each major town along the route giving mileage from the previous town, accumulative mileage for the day and accumulative mileage for the tour in brackets. A summary of available facilities is also given which includes: Tourist Information, Rail Station, Bank, Post Office, Library, Cinema, Theatre, Hospital and Shops. Where Shops are mentioned this indicates that a selection of shops is available and that all requirements are generally available. Cycle shops are mentioned specifically. Available accommodation is listed at all points along the route to enable parties to vary the distances covered during a single day. A detailed route map and relief map is provided and the text gives a full route description with handy hints and additional points of interest to watch out for during the day. Despite the fact that metric units have been around for some time all distances and heights have been quoted in imperial units of miles and feet as on balance I think people are more comfortable with them.

THE ROUTE

Britain is a country rich in diversity. The landscape varies from the flat and fertile to the wild and mountainous. The climate too ranges from sub-tropical in the south-west, wet temperate in the west to dry in the east.

The route forsakes the dramatic granite cliffs of the northern shore for the more pastoral southern coast with its labyrinth of natural harbours, fishing villages and thickly wooded estuaries and visits the towns of Penzance and Truro, both built on the profits of tin and copper. The 19th-century mines now litter the countryside like a ghostly inheritance from the Industrial Revolution. St Austell and Liskeard lead into the county of Devon.

Devon has a far more mellow character than its rugged Cornish neighbour with scatterings of traditional farmsteads on a landscape of rolling hills. At the heart of the county lies the granite mass of Dartmoor, a high plateau rising to a mean height of over 1000ft above sea level. The county provides possibly some of the most difficult cycling on the tour, as local roadbuilders have chosen a more direct approach to construction compared to some of the more mountainous areas of the country where roads tend to follow contour lines and valleys. Despite this the scenery around Dartmoor is very rewarding with extensive views across the whole south-west peninsula. Once the plateau is crossed torturous country lanes lead to the less aggressive wilds of Exmoor and on to Tavistock where timber-framed houses flaunt a wealth gained from the woollen industry.

The arrival of Taunton brings the third county of the tour and the rich farming areas of the south-west. Somerset is sculpted by the escarpments of the Mendips, Quantocks and the Brendon Hills as well as the underground labyrinths of limestone that spawned the spectacular gorge at Cheddar. Historic towns of Bath, Wells and Glastonbury proudly display their architectural splendour and are all worth diversions from the route that now turns north to reach the city of Bristol.

Bristol stands at the estuary of the River Severn - the largest in the country. The impressive water course is followed north into Gloucestershire and the picturesque towns and villages of the Cotswolds. Fertile meadows form a verdant patchwork by the river bank before reaching Tewkesbury between the Cotswolds to the east and the Malvern Hills to the west. The town of Tewkesbury established itself in the 11th century and now displays a well preserved facade of classic Tudor timber-fronted houses.

The route continues north along the Severn Valley. The town of Evesham, built on both sides of the meandering River Avon, lies at the head of the plum orchards that line the great vale. The River Severn leads north to the architecturally rich city of Worcester, and on to the heartlands of the Industrial Revolution and the birthplace of industry at the Severn Gorge at Ironbridge in Shropshire. The route now continues along the course of the Severn Valley Railway through the rich wooded hills between Bewdley and Bridgnorth. To the west the Shropshire hills buffet the Welsh border rising in ever increasing ridges to merge with the mountains of Snowdonia.

From the new town of Telford the River Severn is left to find its source in the hills of mid Wales while the route continues north through the rich arable lands of Cheshire, wedged between the rugged mountains of North Wales in the west and the peaks of the Pennines in the east.

On initial inspection the counties of Lancashire and Yorkshire contrive to present a seemingly impassable barrier of urban sprawl. The cities of Liverpool and Manchester hug the banks of the Mersey to the west while the Humber links the North Sea to the towns of Sheffield and Leeds. The central Pennine chain completes the barricade. It is surprising therefore that it is Lancashire that provides the breach and offers some of the most diverse and interesting scenery of the tour. The area is a unique mix of quaint rural villages of stone-built cottages and twisted iron monuments which serve as a constant reminder to the industrial heritage. The landscape changes abruptly in the north of the county as the limestone ridges that shape the hillsides of the Dales sweep down to the coast at Morecambe. Full advantage is taken of the local cycle routes which are followed along the country lanes, through the Forest of Bowland before joining the eastern leg of the Cumbrian Cycle Way at Kirkby Lonsdale. The rolling hills of the Pennines are followed to within sight of Hadrian's Wall, before leading into Scotland at the historic blacksmiths shop and toll house at Gretna Green.

The northern coast of the Solway Firth is abundant in heather and gorse that thrives in the predominantly sandy soil. Views across the Solway Firth to the mountains of the Lake District silhouetted against the setting sun are unforgettable. Red sandstone is plentiful and is found widely in the local architecture with fine examples in the historic town of Dumfries.

A local cycle route is followed north through some of the most picturesque scenery in Scotland to reach the town of Sanquhar at the junction of the Southern Upland Way. This charming section continues through New Cumnock and on to Kilmarnock where a local Sustran cycle route leads pleasantly north along delightful backroads, canal paths and disused rail routes before delivering the unwary cyclist to the industrialised banks of the River Clyde.

The Erskine Bridge provides the route across this famous river from where a further cycleway leads north along the banks of the River Leven to the shores of Britain's largest loch at Balloch. Loch Lomond's eastern bank is followed for its 24-mile length to Crianlarich where the meandering road traces the course of the West Highland Way into the Highlands, and across Rannoch Moor and into Glen Coe - historic site of the slaughter of the MacDonald clan in 1692.

Fort William stands in the shadow of Britain's largest mountain Ben Nevis, at a point where the Caledonian Canal flows into the waters of Loch Eil and Loch Linnhe. The highlands of Scotland have been formed by a violent series of geological events resulting in a chaotic but diverse infusion of rock types. Ancient sediments lie alongside the explosion of metamorphic rocks presenting the landscape with a cloak of diversity that it displays with pride.

A massive geological fault splits the country along a north-easterly line and gives rise to a chain of lochs, of which the most famous is Loch Ness. Once on the east coast the route negotiates the massive incisions of the Beauly and Cromarty Firths with spectacular views back to the Grampian mountains seen across the Moray Firth. From this point the high peaks are left behind for the undulating course that typifies any coastal route to the town of Wick and finally to the headland of John O'Groats.

PLANNING

One of the secrets behind any successful tour lies in adequate preparation - plus a bit of luck. Many cyclists, however, would disagree with this viewpoint, preferring instead to set off on a tour with the bare minimum of planning, accepting anything that the adventure may present. There is absolutely nothing wrong with this view providing it is accepted that the adventure may include arriving at a hostel only to find it is fully booked or lengthy delays caused by a simple breakdown that had not been foreseen. Too much planning on the other hand can also, in many people's opinion, make a tour a little too sterile. A trip where every eventuality is catered for may even be a slight anticlimax. The main advantage to the planning of any tour of this nature is to maximise the use of the time available. Good planning will reduce frustrating delays and allow more time to simply enjoy the trip.

Requirements for planning will be different depending on the type of accommodation chosen, whether a back-up vehicle will be used, level of fitness, time available etc. This guidebook has been written to provide a framework of information from which individuals may tailor an itinerary suited to themselves.

The text lists each type of accommodation available along the route with more detailed description of availability at the daily stops utilised in the guide. One of the first decisions to make regarding the tour logistics is whether or not to undertake the trip as a self-sufficient unit. This can mean with or without the use of a support vehicle. Obviously the choice of equipment would be very different if all the gear was carried by the riders as compared with the use of a support vehicle. An alternative to "going it alone" would be to take advantage of the growing number of organisations that offer a tour management service. This could include the transport of all equipment, the provision of all meals and may even include a breakdown service along the route. Such a service is offered for the Lands End to John O'Groats route by Bike Events. This method may not appeal to the purist but is a good way for individuals to meet other cyclists. It also has the advantage that minimal equipment is carried allowing greater freedom and mobility for the riders. It also offers security in the knowledge that help is always at hand to overcome any problem that may be encountered.

ACCOMMODATION

The type of accommodation required varies from the basic campsite to the luxury hotel. When planning individual requirements it is worth noting that accommodation offered through cycling magazines has the advantage of being geared to the needs of the tourer. Such a landlady is less likely to cast horrified looks when two cyclists arrive after a 50-mile day in the pouring rain. It is quite probable that drying facilities, a warm drink and a sympathetic ear are not far away.

Camping
Camping provides the ultimate in touring freedom and flexibility, particularly if all the equipment is carried by the riders. Touring sites are plentiful and one or two lightweight cycle tourers can usually be squeezed in the corner of any crowded campsite. The only restriction applies to larger groups where it is advisable to book ahead in order to guarantee a place. This is especially true during high season.

The main disadvantage of this method of travel is the considerable weight penalty that comes from carrying all your own gear. A heavily laden bike can be a difficult beast to master and choice of equipment must be a major consideration. A suggested equipment list has been provided in the appropriate section of this guide.

The standard of touring campsites in Britain has been gradually improving over recent years and facilities are falling in line with continental sites. Campsites are abundant throughout Britain and vary considerably in price depending on the facilities offered. A shower is probably one of the most essential and all campsites referred to in this guide are equipped with flush toilets and showers.

Wild campsites are plentiful in rural areas and make a pleasant change from institutionalised sites. Permission should always be obtained from the landowners who are, more often than not, only too pleased to show hospitality. Special care should be taken to clear the site before leaving.

Bed and Breakfast
Bed and breakfast is as popular as ever and most towns and villages throughout the country offer some form of overnight accommodation. Standards are improving with a gradual increase in facilities on offer. This has brought with it the inevitable price increase. Budget, down to earth accommodation is still available although becoming rarer. Many establishments are non-smoking and some offer only vegetarian food. Any restrictions on houses mentioned in the text has been highlighted.

Youth Hostel

Hostel touring offers a lightweight alternative to camping. Hostels are extensively distributed and offer the tourer flexibility at a reasonable price without the excessive weight penalty that comes with cycle touring. The Youth Hostel Association now allows up to three consecutive nights' stay which allows greater freedom on wet days. This accommodation is popular with cyclists and backpackers and provides friendly and communal overnight stops with the chance to share the day's experiences with other travellers. Details of available hostels along the route have been given in the relevant section of the guide and prebooking is advisable in high season. Full details can be obtained from the Youth Hostel Association.

Many establishments now offer self-contained family accommodation.

WHEN TO GO

It would be nice to be able to predict a period of stable weather for which to plan such a tour. However the pattern of the weather in the British Isles is not straightforward and a certain amount of pot luck has to be taken. Traditionally the summer season is considered to cover July and August. Statistically these are the hottest months of the year with all facilities, including accommodation, available to the tourist. These are also the most popular months for annual holidays resulting in general overcrowding of roads, tourist areas and amenities etc. June and September are quieter months and June has the added advantage of longer daylight hours. Fine cycling conditions may also be found in May and October although accommodation availability may be less widespread. In truth a period of settled weather may occur at any time throughout the year.

Fitness

One of the most important aspects of preparation concerns rider fitness. If it is the intention to follow the suggested route in the guide it is advisable that riders are capable of completing the required distances. A distance of 50 miles is not beyond the capability of most riders if it is taken in isolation, however to complete this distance over many consecutive days requires some form of training if only to become "saddle fit". It is suggested that a single ride of no less than two-thirds of the expected daily distance is cycled twice a week for the month preceding the tour. It is best to build up to this distance over a period leading up to the preceding month. It is important for the enjoyment of the trip to establish an adequate level of fitness and these training runs provide a good opportunity to test out equipment and to find a cycling rhythm that will all add to the enjoyment and the success of the trip.

MAPS

The ideal scale of map from which to cycle tour is 1:50,000. This gives plenty of detail but each sheet still covers an acceptable area in which to plan individual tours. For the purpose of this tour this scale of map is impractical as the number required to cover the total area is prohibitive. The guide provides maps covering the daily route plans to a scale of 4 miles to 1 inch, but it is advisable to carry a more detailed plan to facilitate excursions from the described route as well as covering the eventuality of losing the route. The maps provided do not have as much general detail about the surrounding area. Ordnance Survey market a selection of motoring maps drawn to a scale of 3 miles to 1 inch or $1^{1}/_{2}$ miles to 1 inch. These maps are cheap and also provide a great deal of detail. Individual pages may be discarded to save weight as they are no longer required. Organised tours will generally provide riders with individual day sheets with information specific to the arrangements of the tour.

HOW TO GET THERE

The remote nature of these two points of the British Isles means that access is not straightforward. Intercity trains run direct from Euston Station in London to Penzance in Cornwall but cycles must be prebooked for which a small charge is made. From Penzance the only way to reach Lands End for the independent traveller is to cycle the 12 miles - an easy first day for those choosing to start at Lands End.

Travel to John O'Groats may also be made by rail with Intercity trains to Inverness from where local connections can be taken to Helmsdale, Georgemas Junction and Thurso where, again, the 20 miles to John O'Groats must be made by cycle.

The majority of the journey could be made by air with internal flights to either Wick in the north-east or Bristol in the south-west. Wick is serviced by local shuttle flights from Glasgow, Dundee and Edinburgh and transfers can be obtained from Bristol to Penzance.

Road offers the most convenient transfer but for the independent traveller this will involve a rendezvous with a generous friend or relative. The tour still attracts media attention and this could be used to tempt a local business into providing the pick-up and drop-off vehicle in exchange for a little free advertising.

THE BICYCLE

The selection of different cycle types available is bewildering, however there are specific qualities built into the design of a bike that are best suited to distance touring and will therefore enhance the rider's safety and enjoyment of a tour of this length. It is assumed that anybody planning a cycle tour of this distance will have had a fair degree of experience and would already have a bike or would have at least a good idea of the type of cycle required. Any modern cycle will, with the minimum of maintenance, give thousands of miles of trouble-free service and therefore any modern cycle would be capable of completing the tour. Despite this it is still worth considering the advantages that a specialised touring mount can offer. This is particularly true if it is intended for the bike to be heavily laden. In general, features to look out for are a frame of Chrome-Moly steel with aluminium components throughout. I have attempted to list the features more applicable to the tourer.

Any choice of bicycle for the majority of cyclists is a compromise based on:

1) Intended use - this will usually determine the budget allocation.

2) Personal preferences.

3) Money - the cost of a custom-built touring bike is considerable and beyond the resources of all but the most dedicated tourers but it is worth remembering that, as a general rule, the more expensive the equipment the better the quality. This is true to the point where equipment becomes over-specialised.

So what is there to look for? The advice must always be buy the best you can afford!

The major considerations for the cycle tourer are (and not

necessarily in this order):-

1) Strength - The design must be rigid with a positive, predictable handling under heavy loads. The gearing must cover a wide range to increase hill-climbing capabilities.

2) Reliability - The reliability of a cycle is achieved by a good initial purchase and a sound maintenance policy.

3) Comfort and Safety - This can be optimised by the correct choice of equipment. The bike must be capable of accepting the many accessories required such as water carriers, mudguards etc. The wheels should be robust with the capability of fitting a wide diameter tyre for extra comfort.

The popularity of the ATB (mountain bike) has extended its influence into the design of all cycles. Most manufacturers still produce a purpose-built touring bike that incorporates all the essential features. At first impression the ATB may seem ideally suited to the task. It is rugged with ample gearing capability and robust braking. But wheel sizes, frame size and riding position combine to produce a tiring road tourer. A new breed of hybrids are now available that incorporate some of the ATB features with a more traditional size frame and wheels.

The Frame

The most important factors to consider when choosing a cycle frame are the material and the size. The frame is the skeleton of the bike and determines the characteristics of handling, response etc. High strength seamless drawn tubing of alloy steel (Reynolds 531 or 501) is universally accepted as the best construction material, offering probably the best combination of durability, strength, weight and responsiveness. As a general rule the better quality the frame the lighter the bike will be for a given strength.

The size of the frame is given as the length of the seat tube. British frames are still measured in inches and are available in $1/2$ inch increments. A good rule of thumb is to measure the inside leg and deduct 8 inches to give the required frame size. This should allow the rider to stand astride the top tube (cross bar) with feet flat on the ground.

One of the most important exercises that is often neglected is the correct adjustment of the riding position. This will often highlight an incorrect frame size.

Wheels and Tyres

The next most important components in the make-up of a good touring cycle are the wheels and tyres. Wheels are generally constructed of either steel or alloy and are available in a variety of sizes. 700c is the present standard and is recommended for its wide availability of spares. Aluminium wheels are more expensive than steel but of better quality, and fitted with quick release hubs offer greater convenience for repair but, of course, are more vulnerable to theft. Most standard wheels have 32 spokes but to cope with the extra weight carried by a touring cycle it is advisable to have a rear wheel with extra spokes. The spokes themselves are either made of steel or stronger stainless steel. Double butted spokes offer extra strength at the point of maximum stress without any appreciable weight penalty. Higher strength spokes of 13 Standard Wire Gauge (SWG) are recommended.

Rims are also constructed from steel or aluminium alloy with the box section construction offering the greatest strength. The wheel rim should be capable of taking a wide section tyre.

Tyres are a compromise between a smaller cross section tyre that gives smooth road running and a larger cross section that gives greater reliability, resistance to punctures and high road shock absorption. For most situations tyre inflation and rubber composition have more effect on roadholding than tyre tread. It is for these reasons that a tyre section of less than 32mm is not recommended for a tour of this type.

Any bike equipped for serious touring should be fitted with full length mudguards.

Brakes

There are three principal types of brake: the side pull, centre pull and cantilever. The centre pull design is marginally more efficient, and requires less adjustment than the side pull and is therefore popular with tourers. Performance of the cantilever design is superior to the first two in all respects, having both a greater mechanical advantage and a better balance. This design of brake is a standard fitting to all

ATBs, hybrids and serious touring bikes.

Pedals, Crank and Gearing

Muscular injuries are rare among cyclists due to the low impact nature of the exercise. The knee joint is probably the most vulnerable area and can be overloaded as a result of using a too high gear. Cyclists should aim to maintain a comfortable and even pedalling rate (cadence) of over 60rpm. This cadence is then maintained over a variety of terrain and the loading should be varied by the use of gears. As a guide a tourer will be looking to maintain a cadence of greater than 55 on a fully laden cycle.

Almost all modern cycles employ a derailleur gear system. The pedals are connected to a chainring that drives a rear sprocket set and the gear ratio is selected by a mechanism that derails the chain onto a selection of rear sprockets. The gear ratio is still, rather quaintly, expressed in inches and is dependent on the number of teeth in the chainring, the number of teeth in the rear sprocket and the size of the rear wheel. The ratio is given as the distance travelled after one revolution of the pedals. ATBs offer a greater selection of gear ratios than ever before, employing 3 chainrings and 7 sprockets giving a selection of 21 ratios. Most tourers offer 10 and it is often perfectly adequate to select from 5. It is important to remember that gears cannot do the hard work for you and are no substitute for legpower. It is not how many ratios that are available but over what range these ratios operate that is important to the tourer. A bike having 21 gears will have a lot more overlap of ratios than a bike having only 5. This is again a compromise between gear range and smoothness of operation because the ratios cannot be too far apart as the derailleur system cannot change smoothly between one and another. It is also harmful to the mechanics of the derailleur drive system to run the chain from the large front chainring to the large rear sprocket or from the smaller chainring to the smallest rear sprocket as this mode of operation produces excessive chain wear.

The following figures show typical values for a touring bike and an ATB.

The touring bike will have a chainring of 52 and 48 and a freewheel selection of 13, 16, 19, 22 and 30.

The mountain bike will have a chainring of 48, 38 and 28 with a freewheel selection of 14, 16, 17, 22, 24 and 28.

As can be seen, although the ATB has a greater selection of ratios the range is not in fact as great as the touring set.

A cotterless crank should be chosen to transfer the drive from the pedals to the gear system. Cotterless cranks are generally made of alloy and due to the construction are relatively maintenance free. They are lighter than steel cranks employing cotterpin fastenings and also less prone to failure. The system is also marginally more efficient. However this method of construction necessitates a special tool to remove the crank nut.

Toe clips are an essential addition to the drive system. Their usefulness lies not, as is commonly thought, in the assistance to the turning motion of the pedals on the upward stroke but purely in maintaining the feet firmly on the pedals and therefore eliminating wasted energy expelled by the rider in keeping them there.

The Seat
Choose a seat that is as comfortable as possible. This is largely a matter of personal choice so shop around. Adjustment of riding position also plays a very important part in rider comfort.

Handlebars
The dropped handlebar is still one of the most popular styles as it offers a variety of riding positions which is very important over a long distance ride. The dropped position is useful against headwinds while the cruise position offers a relaxing alternative over easier sections of the route. A popular riding position on dropped bars is semi-crouched on the brake hoods. This proves very comfortable over a distance ride. The handlebar comfort can be further improved by the use of closed cell plastic foam fitted to the bars. Aluminium is used to make handlebars in all but the cheapest models.

Lights and Lighting
On a tour of this nature it is unlikely that any distance will be covered after dark. However it is advisable to be equipped for travelling after dark to:

   a) Aid visibility in poor weather conditions
   b) Cover short trips out from overnight accommodation into

nearby towns

c)   Use as nightlights when camping or staying in hostels.

When cycling in built-up areas the priority is to be seen whereas in more rural situations, lights are often obligatory to see your way around.

The ideal system that covers the needs of the first two situations is the fixed dynamo. Dynamos are cheap and easy to fit and lighting is available whenever it is required but has the disadvantage of not working when the bike is stationary. Although this is not illegal it can be potentially dangerous. Many systems are available that automatically switch to a back-up battery if the bike is stationary. Dynamos are available in two styles:

1)   The bottle type that runs off the sidewall of the tyre and

2)   The cylindrical type which is fitted to the bottom bracket and runs off the tyre tread.

The bottle type is the cheaper of the two but both give a good output and are very reliable except in wet conditions when both types are prone to slipping on the tyre. The output of the units depends on the speed of the bike, and voltage regulation is usually crude which necessitates carrying a good supply of spare bulbs.

Despite the fact that cycle lamps have been available nearly as long as the bicycle there still appears to be some difficulty in the manufacture of a reliable design that combines with a long battery life. Rechargeable batteries have too short a capacity to be useful in cycle lamps. The output from battery lamps is very good but care should be taken when choosing a mounting position that the lamp is not obscured by baggage. The clamp arrangement that is common with this type of lamp can be potentially dangerous if fitted to oval section forks. Cycle lamps also have the disadvantage that they are very attractive to thieves.

Accessories
A pump is an essential item to have at all times. There are now models available that double up as locks, although how efficiently it carries out both tasks is debatable.

Additional items that are useful include cycle lock, water bottle, speedometer, milometer, mirrors and reflectors.

Adjustment of Riding Position
The riding position must be adjusted in order to give maximum riding efficiency and maximum comfort.

1) The height of the seat is correct when the leg is straight with the crank in line with the down tube. If the frame size is correct this should give a 2-4 inch projection of the seat pillar from the seat tube (fig. 1).
2) The fore and aft adjustment of the seat is given with the crank at $^1/_4$ turn. The knee should be directly above the pedal (fig. 2).
3) This adjustment is checked in the dropped position when the knee should brush the elbow as shown (fig. 3).

BAGS AND BAGGAGE
It is always best to load the cycle and not the cyclist. The load needs to be as low as possible in order to keep the centre of gravity low. This will minimise the effect of the extra weight on the handling characteristics of the cycle. For a tour of this nature low mounted front and rear panniers should carry the bulk of equipment. The cycle rack at the back can be used for bulky items such as a tent whilst a handlebar bag is ideal for small items required for the day's riding. The weight must be spread between the front and rear of the cycle with the bias to the rear. Cycle baggage is made from hard wearing material but it is NOT waterproof, despite what the salesman may have told you. Seams are generally not sealed and provide a path for water to enter. It is best to store ALL equipment in waterproof bags inside the panniers. Ensure all baggage is securely fastened to the bike. The extra weight will increase the speed of the freewheel downhill and a pannier falling into the front wheel, downhill at 40mph is no fun. The handling characteristics and breaking capacity of the bike will change quite noticeably on a fully loaded cycle and is something to be aware of when starting the tour.

CLOTHING
The general requirement for touring is to wear clothing that is light, comfortable and functional. Cycle shops are adorned with multi-coloured lycra available in a variety of figure hugging designs that will, unless you are fortunate enough to sport the perfect athletic shape, make you cringe with embarrassment. The philosophy behind

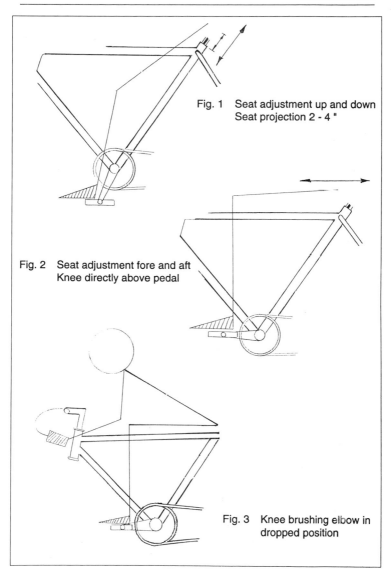

Fig. 1 Seat adjustment up and down
Seat projection 2 - 4 "

Fig. 2 Seat adjustment fore and aft
Knee directly above pedal

Fig. 3 Knee brushing elbow in
dropped position

this equipment is sound. The clothing designs provide light, close fitting layers that offer a flexible system to cope with the cyclist's varying insulation requirements. Close fitting clothing prevents annoying flapping on those fast downhill runs while elongated shirt tails and shorts provide insulation for vulnerable areas. Close fitting lycra shorts should be high-waisted to insulate the lower back and be constructed of six panels to prevent chaffing from seams and have that all important padded seat for extra comfort.

Cycling generates a good deal of heat and any rider should be able to maintain body temperature even on the coldest of days. This does make cyclists vulnerable at rest and for these reasons it is advisable to utilise a layered system of clothing. The standard three-layer system of clothing adopted universally by other outdoor activities should include a Base (Thermal) Layer of comfortable lightweight garment designed to keep moisture away from the skin. A Mid Layer should provide the majority of the insulation requirement. Garments should be close fitting to aid insulation and quick drying. A zip front will aid ventilation but may be uncomfortable in the cycling position. The final layer is the Shell Layer. This is designed to protect the Mid Layer from anything that will impair the insulating quality. This includes wind and rain. Due to the windage caused by cycle travel this aspect of the clothing system is much more important than normal. Also as a result of the increase in body heat output during periods of hard cycling heavy breathable fabrics are tested to the limit of performance and it is often better not to use them. Modern lightweight versions designed specifically for cyclists are improving the situation but are, as always, very expensive. An alternative to this is the good old-fashioned cycle cape. This has many advantages over other waterproofs. It offers good protection with good ventilation and it does not restrict movement. It is also cheaper for similar performance because the material has no breathable quality and hence can be made 100% waterproof. It can also afford some protection to baggage.

Footwear needs to be close fitting and comfortable with a strong sole to spread the pedal load. A narrow fit is also an advantage when using toe clips. Purpose-made cycling shoes are ideal but are difficult to walk in. Laces should be kept short or tucked in to prevent them being caught in the pedals or the chainring. Overshoes offer the luxury of dry feet on those wet days. Breathable fabrics are ideal but expensive. A cheaper alternative would be a couple of plastic bags inside the shoes.

On a tour of this length serious consideration should be given to wearing a helmet. Over half the cycling accidents involving motor vehicles involve injuries to the cyclist's head. The cyclist is more vulnerable to accident on fast descents or in busy traffic although an accident can happen anywhere.

Padded cycling gloves offer a good deal of extra comfort on a ride of this length, as well as additional warmth to the hands, and are well worth considering.

MAINTENANCE

This section does not intend to provide a comprehensive guide to maintenance techniques. This is covered in far more detail in other more specialised publications. The aim of this section is to suggest a series of checks that should be made before embarking on a tour of this nature and to impress the importance of general cycle maintenance. The section also lists some suggested spares and tools that are recommended to be carried and outlines some emergency maintenance techniques that may be useful on the road.

General Cycle Checks
The single greatest factor that reduces reliability is lack of use. No use is probably a greater destroyer of cycles than misuse - this applies not only to cycles but also to riders as well.

Regular cleaning is possibly the single most important contribution to cycle maintenance. By guarding against the build-up of salt, dirt and other potentially corrosive materials the deterioration of a number of exposed components can be prevented. Hot, soapy water is the best cleaning agent.

Regular inspections are also a simple but important tool in preventative maintenance. Components that have safety implications should be given priority. These include brakes, steering and tyres.

Lubrication is the other important preventative maintenance technique. The smooth running of the cycle depends on the free running of the many bearing surfaces. Light lubricants are better than heavy greases in all but the most severe conditions as grease has the tendency to attract dirt and grit which creates an abrasive compound that increases the wear on the bearing surfaces. All bearings on the cycle should be checked periodically for lubrication of the bearing surfaces.

The Chain

The chain is probably the single most vulnerable component on the cycle. It must withstand the highest mechanical stresses in the drive system while at the same time being exposed to the worst conditions. The chain requires regular cleaning. Scrub each link using a toothbrush and a penetrating agent (WD40) to remove all signs of dirt and corrosion. Afterwards lubricate well with a recommended chain lubricant. The chain should always sound smooth in operation with no squeaking.

The remainder of the drive system should also be smooth running. The derailleur should be free from a build-up of grease and dirt and the jockey pulleys should be free running. Changes of gearing should also be smooth and the extreme ratios should be checked to see that the chain is not thrown off the sprocket. Check the operation of the chainwheel change. The freewheel should be free running and the pawl should freely engage when the drive is applied to the system.

Cables

Cables are also susceptible but require nothing more than a regular injection of a light penetrating lubricant down the cable sheath to maintain it in good serviceable condition. Checks should be made for fraying at the cable ends and where the cable enters the sheath. The operation should be smooth.

Wheels

Tyres should be checked for general condition. The rubber shouldn't be perished and there should be no cuts, abrasion or undue wear to the tread pattern. The wheel should be true and all spokes should be in place and of an even tightness.

General

Checks should be made on the tightness of all nuts, bolts and screws on the cycle. A long day's ride may loosen a nut and bolt and a potential equipment failure can be averted by this simple routine. It is a good idea to fit split or shakeproof washers to all cycle fastenings to prevent this gradual loosening. Carriers, mudguards, lights, dynamos and other accessories are most at risk.

EMERGENCY MAINTENANCE TECHNIQUES

It is almost inevitable that some form of breakdown will occur over a tour of this length although if all the above checks are carried out regularly throughout the journey this will certainly go a long way to reducing the probability. One of the best ways to prepare for a breakdown is to arm yourself with a sound working knowledge of the bicycle. This will enable you to assess any failure and decide on the best course of action. Over the route described in the guide a repair is required only to make the bike ridable to the next town where a more lasting repair can be effected.

The type of failure may range from broken spokes resulting in a buckled wheel to a detached freewheel. Drastic failures call for drastic cures. A buckled wheel may be straightened using a drain, a fence or by standing on it. A bearing that has broken up may be temporarily packed with cloth and filled with suntan lotion for lubrication. Even a puncture can be overcome by stuffing cloth into the tyre in place of the inner tube although it is recommended to carry a puncture repair kit. Remember - ingenuity is the key to mobility!

A component will usually give some warning prior to failure. This may manifest itself in a rattle, a squeak or a knocking. The handling may feel different to normal or something may start rubbing. Any abnormality should be investigated immediately.

SUGGESTED SPARES AND TOOL KIT

When considering the tools required to be taken on a trip such as this many factors must be examined. The tool kit required by a solo rider using no back-up, riding a route that takes in some of the more remote parts of the country, will require a more comprehensive kit than a group of riders using main roads with vehicle back-up. Weight must also be a consideration if the riders are to carry all the equipment on the bike. It is pointless carrying spares for jobs that are not intended to be carried out - ie. don't carry a full set of spokes unless it would be your intention to build a wheel by the roadside (which I doubt). Tools and spares should be limited to items required to keep the bike going. As long as the cycle is mobile a repair shop can be reached. The vulnerable areas therefore are tyres, wheels, pedals, chain; in other words the cycle's drive components. Anything else is only a nicety.

Punctures are both common and easily repairable. Therefore a small puncture repair kit is essential. It is also worth taking a spare inner tube in case a valve decides to tear (an almost impossible repair).

Tyre levers (plastic are least aggressive) - three is normal but two will do. Reversible head screwdriver and allen keys are always useful to check the bike over each night.

A single cycle spanner incorporating many sizes of open-ended spanners looks wonderful until it comes to using it. A better idea is to take a small (6 inch) adjustable spanner to cover the majority of the work, with the cycle spanner to hold the occasional spinning nut.

A spare cable can be useful although it is rare that the failure of a single cable can immobilise a cycle to the extent that it can't reach the next cycle shop.

A 14mm socket spanner/pedal extractor is useful, as is a chain breaker and split link. It is advisable to leave space for a selection of cable ties as these are useful for repairing a multitude of component failures on a temporary basis.

Major difficulties can never be planned for and it is inevitable that whatever component is left out is the one that will fail, but if all the basics are catered for, the bike can be kept mobile.

We once came across a cyclist in the north of Scotland who had a trailer rigged up to a tricycle. The machine was so heavily laden with spares that progress on the trip was half that which the cyclist had planned.

SAFETY

Safety of both cycle and rider is always an important consideration when planning a tour. Safety is a factor that influences every aspect of the tour from cycle maintenance to route planning and from equipment selection to choice of clothing. It is each rider's individual responsibility to consider safety. I have endeavoured to indicate specific areas of importance in the text under the relevant sections but it remains up to each cyclist to assess the degree of importance that is given to each point. Remember that the most enjoyable tour of all is a safe one.

I am devoting a few lines to another very important aspect of cycle touring and that is riding techniques. The cyclist must abide by the same rules as any other road user. This includes traffic lights, road signs etc. A cyclist may feel in danger and may as a consequence resort to the use of kerbs, inside lanes etc. to increase the feeling of security or simply to aid progress. This makes the cyclist a very unpredictable creature to all other road users and consequently a very vulnerable one. Be alert at all times and indicate your intentions clearly. The fully laden bike is a more visible and more predictable beast and as such is afforded a little more respect by other road users. Traffic will tend to leave an overtaking width proportional to the size of the vehicle being overtaken, consequently a fully laden cycle is afforded greater courtesy than a solo mount.

In traffic the answer is to ride positively but defensively. Always think the worst; that way you may be some way prepared for it when it happens. It is little consolation to be in the right when it will always be the cyclist who comes off worse from any "close encounter". Try to ride as predictably as possible and to give every other road user a chance of recognising your intentions. Be wary of being forced to ride the gutter run. This is the area of no man's land between the kerb and the road where every motorist thinks every cyclist should be. There are many hazards here for the cyclist including drains, road markings, chippings, spillages etc., all of which are particularly dangerous in wet conditions.

Colourful bright clothing, lights, and reflective strips do not make the cyclist safe. They can, however, increase the chances of other road users seeing you. The key to safe riding is to be vigilant and alert to everything that is going on around you. Be aware of traffic situations and respond to them sensibly. The onus is on the cyclist because it is always the cyclist that has most to lose.

Be safe, be happy and have fun!

Bon Voyage!

The rocky headland at Lands End and the starting point for the tour

View west to the Dartmoor plateau with gradients that typify
the cycling terrain
The river Ribble near Clitheroe on the North Lancashire Cycle Way

The Devil's Bridge at Kirkby Lonsdale
The 12th-century Pendragon Castle believed to have been the home of
Uther Pendragon, the father of King Arthur

DAY 1: LANDS END to PAR

Total Distance: **56 miles**
Cycling Time: **4 hours 30 minutes**

The day provides a gentle introduction to the tour through the picturesque lanes of Cornwall. The south-west peninsula is the most popular holiday destination in Britain and as such the narrow, tree-lined roads that are characteristic of the area can become rather congested during the peak holiday period. Accommodation may also need to be prebooked during high season to ensure an overnight stop. The route climbs from the granite nose of Lands End to the town of Penzance before continuing along the shores of Mounts Bay to Helston. The Lizard Peninsula is bypassed as the route continues across country to Falmouth and then on to Truro before once more joining the coast at St Austell and the picturesque village of Par Sands situated on St Austell Bay.

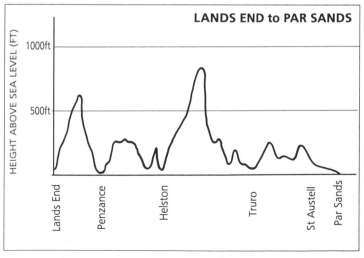

Lands End   0 miles

Campsite: 1^{1}/2m SE on B3315, 1m E on A30.

The tip of the south-west peninsula is indeed a spectacular place: chaotic piles of granite, stacked in picturesque disorder, defiant against the relentless pounding of the Atlantic waves. Over the past few years the character of Lands End has been transformed from an area of rugged natural beauty into a privately owned theme park. The transformation has not deterred the visitors and the site is still one of Cornwall's premier tourist attractions.

Dr Syntax's Head is the true westerly point of the island and will provide the starting point for purists while the steps of the first and last inn is the official starting point for record attempts. A good compromise, if you can afford the entrance fee, is the famous signpost with the daunting inscription "John O'Groats 874 Miles".

The A30 climbs from the Lands End peninsula between stone walls with views extending to both the north and south coasts. Pass through the westernmost village of Sennen with the "First Inn in England" and a small church. Continue along a plateau to pass a turning on the left that descends to the fishing village at Sennen Cove. The landscape has a strong coastal feel with an abundance of gorse and heather lining the route. An ancient hill fort mound is passed on the left at Carn Brea after 6 miles before the route continues on a more undulating course through the villages of Catchall, Drift and Byras Bridge, with overhanging alders and oaks providing welcome shade.

A decorative roundabout marks the outskirts of Penzance from where a right turn leads

steeply downhill into the town.
Continue straight ahead at the
next two roundabouts to
bypass the town with
good views across
Mounts Bay and St
Michael's
Mount.

An alternative route to
this point is to follow
the B3315 south coast road
from Lands End. The route is
more rural and provides easy
access to the area's many picturesque
coves and inlets. It is a popular scenic
route and consequently very busy during
peak holiday season. It has also some steep
ascents and descent at Treen and the Lamorna valley.
The road passes through the villages of Polgigga, Treen,
Trewoofe and Newlyn into Penzance and if time permits it
is certainly a far more picturesque alternative. Total distance
12.9 miles.

Penzance   **9 miles/9 miles**

Campsite: 1m N of Penzance on B3312; Youth Hostel, B&B, Guest
Houses & Hotels.
Tourist Information, Bank, Post Office, Rail Station, Hospital, Cinema,
Cycle Shop, Shops.
*Penzance is the terminus of the Intercity rail connection to the south-west.
The area boasts one of the mildest climates in Britain. Its unique location
supports a variety of sub-tropical plants making the Trengwainton Gardens
one of the most beautiful in the county and a unique attraction for the area.
The town lies in the shelter of Mounts Bay that forms an arc of golden sands
around the majestic granite outcrop of St Michael's Mount. The island is
owned by the National Trust and features an 11th-century monastery and
a 15th-century fort. Access to the island is by boat or causeway at low tide.*

35

St Michael's Mount in Mounts Bay, now owned by the National Trust

Day trips to the Isles of Scilly by boat or helicopter trips along the coast or around the bay are also available.

Leave Penzance on the A30 passing the rail station on the right with a good view on the right, across the bay, to St Michael's Mount. A short dual carriageway leads to a roundabout from where signs for Helston are followed along the A394 at the next roundabout. The road has a wide hard shoulder which allows a relatively safe passage for cyclists and the terrain to Helston provides a pleasant ride. Good picnic spots can be found to the left and right of the road 5 miles out of Penzance. Pass through the villages of Rosudgeon, Germoe and Ashton with good views ahead to the coast at Porthleven before descending into the town of Helston.

Helston   13 miles/22 miles

Campsite: E of town on A394, ¹/₂m S off A3083; B&B, Guest Houses & Hotels.
Bank, Post Office, Hospital, Cinema, Cycle Shop, Shops.
Helston has played an important role in the development of Cornish trade and industry. The old town is an interesting maze of narrow side streets radiating from the central market square. The town is famous for the Flurry Dance Festival that takes place annually on 8th May. The 18th-century parish church of St Michael is very attractive.

Lizard Point is the most southerly point on the British mainland and is situated at the tip of the scenic moorland peninsula of Goonhilly Downs 12 miles south of the town on the A3083. The coastline is particularly beautiful with many picturesque coves of which Mullion Cove on the western shore is probably the best known.

The A394 leads out of Helston signposted "Falmouth and Truro (A39)". The road narrows at Trewennack before widening once more with the provision of a cycle lane. Open views extend across the Cornish countryside littered with the remnants of the mining industry that once thrived here. A short section of dual carriageway leads into Longdowns village which has a campsite, general stores and post office.

Follow the signs to Truro on the A39 to pass numerous roadside picnic sites before commencing the long descent into Perranarworthal alongside the Carrick Roads estuary. The road continues under the shade of trees along a pleasant sheltered section before a steep ascent leads into the city of Truro with its impressive cathedral.

Truro   15 miles/37 miles

Campsite: $3^{1}/2$m W off A390; B&B, Guest Houses & Hotels.
Tourist Information, Bank, Post Office, Cinema, Theatre, Hospital, Rail Station, Cycle Shop, Shops.
The city of Truro is the Cornish administrative centre and is dominated by the three spires of the cathedral. The cathedral was built between 1880 and 1910 and is a fine example of Georgian architecture. It was the first Protestant cathedral to be constructed in England since St Paul's of London in 1675.

The A39 leads through the city and continues north-east towards St Austell. The cycling is generally straightforward with pleasant views to the village of Tresillian. The Holy Trinity church invites closer examination and a general stores and post office has refreshments. The A39 becomes the A390 5 miles out of Truro with the A39 continuing to Bodmin. A sharp left turn and a steep ascent lead out of the village of Probus with rewards of views across to the peaks of Bodmin Moor. One mile from St Austell an 8% descent followed by a gruelling reascent leads into the town.

St Austell   15 miles/52 miles

Campsite: 3m SW on A390, $2^{1}/2$m E on A390; B&B, Guest Houses & Hotels.

Bank, Cinema, Hospital, Post Office, Rail Station, Cycle Shop, Shops. *St Austell has its main industry in the export of china clay used in the manufacture of porcelain. Clay is dug from the surrounding country and shipped from the harbour at Par. Built on a steep slope the town is a warren of narrow backstreets with the market once again forming the focal point.*

The Wheal Martyn China Clay Museum documents the history of the clay works in the area and Roche Rock, 4 miles north of St Austell, is worth a visit if time permits. The granite outcrop is capped with the chapel of St Michael built in 1409 and is spectacular in its oddity.

The A390 is initially signposted for Lostwithiel and then for Liskeard. A series of traffic lights lead out of the town where a turning on the right is taken in about 4 miles for Par.

Par Sands   4 miles/56 miles

Camping: 4m E of St Austell off A3082.
Village Stores.
St Austell Bay stretches from Black Head in the west to Gribbin Head in the east. The sheltered bay typifies the south Cornish scenery with timeless fishing villages nestled on gently shelving beaches of sand.

The South West provides some of the most testing cycling terrain on the tour

DAY 2: PAR to MORETONHAMPSTEAD

Total Distance: **55 miles**
Cycling time: **5 hours 10 minutes**

The route leaves the sanctuary of the coast and strikes out across the wilds of Dartmoor. The ascents and descents gradually become more onerous as the towns of Lostwithiel and Liskeard lead alongside the high ground of Bodmin Moor and into the county of Devon. Tavistock provides a last chance for refreshments before the plateau of Dartmoor Forest is crossed. The fringes of this beautiful wilderness are intertwined with a maze of canopied roads that interconnect to the many villages. Moretonhampstead is the largest town on the eastern fringe of the moor and provides a delightful overnight stop after a tough day in the saddle.

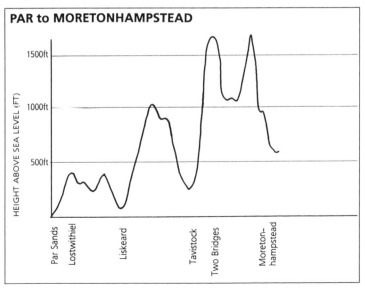

39

Par   **0 miles**   **(56 miles)**

From Par Sands follow the road left to pass under a rail bridge.
Continue over a level crossing turning right before the road begins to
climb. Follow alongside the railway to join the A390 by traffic lights
at St Blazey. Turn right and continue over a series of steep ascents and
descents that characterise the cycling in the south-west of the country.
After 6 miles a final steep descent leads into the Fowey estuary and
the market town of Lostwithiel.

Lostwithiel   **6.2 miles**   **(62.2 miles)**

Campsite: 1¹/₂m SW off A390; B&B, Guest Houses & Hotels.
Tourist Information, Rail Station, Hospital, Post Office, Library,
Shops.
*During the 13th century the town was the capital of Cornwall. The river was
navigable which provided trade routes and the town acted as a trade centre
for the mining industry. The Earls of the time resided in Restormel
Castle which survives today as one of the best preserved castles
of the period. The town has great historic interest with
notable architectural examples from many periods.*

Climb steeply out of the town to
pass the site of Druids Hill on the
right. The terrain begins to relent
and a more gentle
undulating
course is now
followed
through the
villages
of West
Taphouse and
East Taphouse to reach
the junction with the A38. The
road is fringed with steep wooded
slopes and embankments before a short
section of dual carriageway is reached at
Looe Mills. Take the first exit left to Liskeard
town centre.

Liskeard **11.2 miles/17.4 miles**
(73.4 miles)

Campsite: 4m W off A38 on B3360, 2¹/₂m NW off A38; B&B.
Rail Station, Post Office, Bank, Cycle Shop, Shops.

Situated between the wilderness of Bodmin Moor to the north and the coast of the English Channel to the south, Liskeard holds a strong strategic position into Cornwall. As such it has traditionally taken on the role of market centre for the farming community with regular cattle fairs held to this day.

The A390 climbs briefly before descending to cross the River Seaton to the north-east of the town. The small village of Merrymeet offers refreshments on the crest of the hill before a descent is made once more (campsite on the left). The undulating trend continues through St Ive before a giddy wooded descent leads across the River Lynher at Newbridge and into the county of Devon. The steep sided river valley has been of great strategic value through the ages and an ancient burial mound, now owned by the National Trust, can be found a short distance downstream.

A sharp climb once more under the welcome shade of beech and oak leads to Callington. This charming village is now bypassed by the A390 which should be followed for the shortest continuation of the route. Turn right at the first roundabout and straight over the second to continue on the southern slopes of the 1000ft Kit Hill with extensive views north to the rolling hills of the moorland plateau at Bodmin.

The network of villages grouped on the wooded slopes to the west of Tamar provide outstanding cycling country. Pass the railway

41

station at Drakewalls and begin a long descent to cross the Tamar at Hatchwood. A long and gruelling ascent now begins, first shaded and then open to the midday heat, seemingly imprisoned between the high hedgerows either side. Tavistock provides a welcome sight to the weary traveller, situated by the edge of the National Park on the bubbling water of the River Tavy.

Tavistock	**17.6 miles/35 miles**	**(91 miles)**

Campsite: 2m E on B3357, 4m W off A390; Youth Hostel, B&B Guest Houses, Hotel.
Tourist Information, Hospital, Post Office, Bank, Cycle Shop, Shops.
The town is situated beneath the shadow of Dartmoor on the fast flowing River Tavy that drains from the moor. The town grew around the Benedictine Abbey and prospered on the wealth of tin and wool. Sir Francis Drake was born here in 1542. Now the town acts as a touring centre for Dartmoor and as a consequence provides all facilities for the visitor to the area.

The climb from Tavistock up to the Dartmoor plateau is memorable. It differs from other climbs so far encountered on the route in that the road to Dartmoor has been stripped of its camouflage and rises directly ahead. Cross the river and leave Tavistock in an easterly direction on the B3357. The 1000ft climb is over in a few miles from where a beautiful open panorama unfolds.

Dartmoor

The great plateau of rolling moorland extends for over 360 square miles and was designated a National Park in 1951. The area covers most of southern Devon although the focus of the Park is on the central region known as Dartmoor Forest. Most of the rivers of south Devon have their source in the boggy northern end of the moor and many beauty spots are to be found where the water leaves the plateau. Lydford Gorge is a fine example of this type of scenery, situated 5 miles north of Tavistock off the A386. The open grassland is interspersed with granite tors, weathered by centuries to form unique natural sculptures. The average height of the plateau is 1000ft with the highest point of High Willhays rising to over double that. The area was occupied by large numbers of Bronze and Iron Age farmers and many relics from this period are still much in evidence.

Two Bridges marks the point at which the road crosses the West Dart River and takes its name from the stone crossing at the site. Turn left on the B3212 signposted Moretonhampstead and continue past the wooded slopes at Postbridge for about 5 miles to reach a good viewpoint at the north-eastern edge of the moor. The route now changes in character following a course of narrow roads twisting between the high hedgerows as if trapped in a complex natural maze. The ascents and descents gradually relent to deliver a weary cyclist into the town of Moretonhampstead.

Moretonhampstead   20 miles/55 miles   (111 miles)

Camping: $2^{1/2}$m E off B3212; Youth Hostel 4m E on B3212 at Steps Bridge, B&B, Hotel.
Post Office, Shops.
Picturesque town on the eastern fringes of Dartmoor.

One last effort is required to reach the campsite by leaving the town on a narrow road from the market square. Climb steeply from the town around the north of a large hill at Marden Down. A scary descent is then undertaken that tests any cyclist's mental nerve to reach the campsite on the banks of the Teign, $2^{1/2}$ miles from Moretonhampstead.

DAY 3: MORETONHAMPSTEAD to BRIDGWATER

Total Distance:	**58.6 miles**
Cycling Time:	**4 hours 35 minutes**

With the testing terrain of Dartmoor now behind, the tour takes on a more pastoral character. An initial climb from Moretonhampstead provides a reminder that the hills of Devon are not exclusive to the moorland but from the town of Crediton the route picks a winding course through a picturesque Devon often overlooked by the visitor to the west country. Small hamlets, rich in rural charm, litter the upper reaches of the rivers Taw, Yeo and Torridge linked by quaint country lanes that provide a pleasant route through rural England.

Dunkley Beacon is the highest point on the gentler moorland of Exmoor, rising to 1705ft. The route then follows a north-easterly

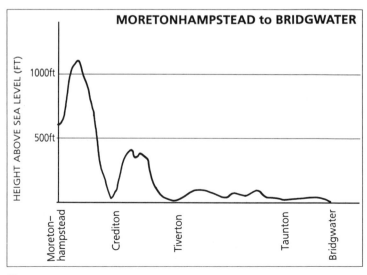

course to pass between the Blackdown Hills in the south and the Quantocks in the north, along the Vale of Taunton to reach the town of Taunton at its head in the county of Somerset. From the cider capital of the west the route turns north to the old maritime town of Bridgwater.

Moretonhampstead   0 miles   (111 miles)

A devious path is now followed across the main A30 to arrive at Crediton. Cross the River Teign and continue straight over at the crossroads to climb from the river valley. The road leads out of the Park boundary into Lanley before descending steeply into Brook. A further climb leads to a left turn that crosses the main A30 and continues into the town of Tedburn St Mary. The winding route continues north along small lanes fringed by deciduous woodland to reach Venny Tedburn (Court Barton). At a T-junction 1 mile from the village turn right and continue to a crossroads where a left turn leads over the River Yeo and under a rail bridge to join the A377 into Crediton.

Crediton   11.1 miles/11.1 miles   (122.1 miles)

Campsite: Cheriton Bishop 5m SW; B&B, Guest Houses & Hotel.
Bank, Post Office, Rail Station, Cycle Shop, Shops.
The large Holy Cross church that dominates the town is the result of Christian influences in the area as early as AD 674. The Chapter House next to the church is one of the few buildings to have survived the great fires of 1743 and 1769 and it has been a meeting place for the church's governors since 1547.

    The A3072 leads out of the town and provides a glorious afternoon's cycling into Tiverton. The road is generally quiet with an ever changing vista of the rolling Devon countryside. Each descent provides just enough momentum to propel the cycle over the crest of the next hill, around the next bend and into the next view.

Tiverton   11.8 miles/22.9 miles   (133.9 miles)

Campsite: Bampton 6m N; B&B.
Tourist Information, Bank, Post Office, Hospital, Cinema, Shops.
Tiverton displays the finery that would be associated with a market town

founded on the wealth of the textile industry, although much of the town's inheritance is from much earlier. St Peter's church dates back to the reign of William the Conqueror and predates the sandstone of Tiverton Castle that was commissioned in the 12th century. The Great Western Canal is a fine example of the large engineering projects that were born out of the industrial wealth created at the turn of the century. Knightshayes Court is situated 2 miles north of Tiverton and was built for the descendants of John Heathcoat who founded the modern textile industry.

The route leaves the town on the A396, passing the castle to reach a roundabout on the A361. Continue straight ahead on the A396 to follow the course of the Exe Valley. The cycling is delightful in a setting of wooded hills and meandering streams. Ahead can be seen glimpses of the Brendon Hills and Exmoor National Park. Exmoor covers 265 square miles and rises on all sides to a plateau of about 1400ft. The scenery is arguably more dramatic where this plateau meets the Bristol Channel in the north to form an abrupt and rugged coastline. However the rolling grasslands and heather moors that cover the southern extremes possess a tranquil charm that typifies

this corner of England.

Continue for 5 miles before joining the B3227 to Bampton. Turn left to cross the River Bathern into Bampton and at the T-junction by the church turn right again to follow the river course in the shadow of steep sided hills to reach Shillingford. The road continues more easily to pass through Waterrow and

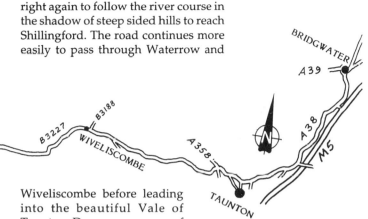

Wiveliscombe before leading into the beautiful Vale of Taunton Deane - an area of rolling farmland, famous for the cider apples that flourish in its fertile soils.

The road joins the A358 to reach a roundabout. Continue straight ahead along a steep embankment and continue into the town centre.

Taunton   26.4 miles/49.3 miles   (160.3 miles)

Campsite: 2m NE on A38, 4m SE off A358; B&B, Guest Houses & Hotel.

Tourist Information, Bank, Post Office, Hospital, Cinema, Theatre, Cycle Shop, Shops.

Taunton is a fine example of a period town situated on the River Tone to the south of the Quantock Hills and north of the Black Down Hills. The unique sheltered location of the beautiful Vale of Taunton gives rise to the fertile soil responsible for Taunton Cider. The town has much historic interest with the castle dating back to Norman times and many fine examples of Georgian architecture that impart a style and elegance to the high street typical of the period.

The town provided the stage for the uprising by the Duke of Monmouth during the civil war and bore witness to the eventual execution of the survivors of the resulting battle of Sedgemoor.

Pass the church to leave the town north-east on the A3259 to Monkton Heathfield before joining the A38 on a section of dual carriageway. Follow this for about a mile where the road turns north to run parallel with the M5 into the town of North Petherton. To the west rise the peaks of the Quantock Hills that separate the Vale of Taunton Deane from the Somerset Plain and Sedgemoor.

This vast fertile area south of the Mendips is criss-crossed by a grid-like network of roads and land drains. The towns in the area make use of natural high ground and the A39 itself follows a course east to Glastonbury along the line of the Polden Hills. The cycling across this area is straightforward with the Mendip Hills in the distance providing the next barrier to surmount in the path north. The Quantock Hills in the west form a fine upland ridgeway and offer extensive views.

From North Petherton the A38 leads into Bridgwater.

Bridgwater   9.3 miles/58.6 miles   (169.6 miles)

Campsite: 3¹/₂m NE off A39, ¹/₂m S on A38; B&B.
Tourist Information, Rail Station, Bank, Post Office, Hospital, Cinema, Theatre, Cycle Shop, Shops.

Bridgwater is situated at the estuary of the River Parrett. The town was a key port for the industries in the south-west, the Great Western Canal providing the link for the mining and textile industries with the sea. Bristol is responsible for the demise of the town's role in modern industry and the quayside is today lined with shops. The town has a 13th-century castle and a 14th-century church. To the east rise the Polden Hills and the low-lying plains of Sedgemoor. The site held the last battle to be fought on English soil in 1685 and was the scene of the Duke of Monmouth's failed uprising in the English civil war.

The "First and Last" house in Scotland at Gretna Green and the
blacksmiths that witnessed many runaway marriages
The old gatehouse in the grounds of Drumlanrig Castle

The Erskine bridge spanning the river Clyde
The route into the Highlands along the banks of Loch Lomond

DAY 4: BRIDGWATER to STROUD

Total Distance: **65.4 miles**
Cycling Time: **5 hours**

From the foot of the Mendip Hills a choice of routes can be followed. The first continues north to cross the hills and continues on to Bristol from where a gentle course is followed in Gloucestershire to reach the town of Stroud overlooking the Vale of Berkeley in the heart of the Cotswolds. The alternative is more picturesque and explores the gorge at Cheddar before detouring south-east around the Mendips to visit the historic centres of Wells and Bath, finally continuing along the border of Wiltshire and Avon into the Cotswolds and on to Stroud. Whichever itinerary is chosen the scenic splendour of the area will ensure a memorable day's cycling.

Bridgwater   **0 miles**   **(169.6 miles)**

The A38 leaves the town north, fringed with the hardy grasses and abandoned boats that impress a coastal flavour which is often reinforced by the biting wind that cuts in from the Bristol Channel.

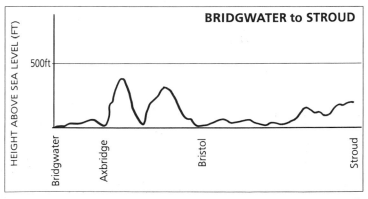

The area is quite exposed with open farmland stretching as far as the eye can see. The cycling is physically easy but the exposed nature of the area would make for a miserable ride in adverse conditions. The villages of Dunball, Pawlett, Huntspill and Highbridge provide welcome reminders that progress is being made.

Brent Knoll stands to the north of Burnham-on-Sea and rises to over 400ft overlooking the Channel. The site is now owned by the National Trust and was originally an ancient hill fort.

At the fork in the road continue along the A38 to reach the town of Axbridge on the edge of the Mendips.

Axbridge   14.9 miles   (184.5 miles)

Camping: 1m E off B371, ¹/₂m E on A31, 2¹/₂m SE on A371 at Cheddar. Village Stores, Post Office.

Axbridge is a small village located at the foot of the Mendips and serves as a popular touring base for exploring the area.

The Mendips

The Mendip Hills are a fine example of limestone upland scenery. The hills only rise to the modest altitude of 1000ft although the rounded tops provide magnificent viewpoints across the Severn Estuary and the vast Plains of Salisbury.

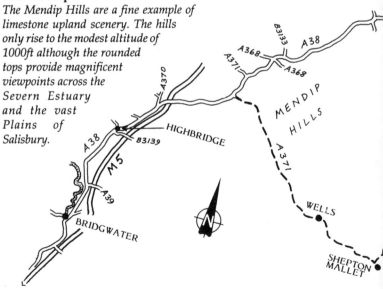

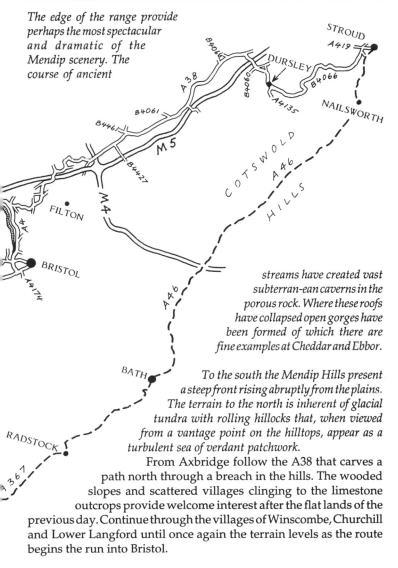

The edge of the range provide perhaps the most spectacular and dramatic of the Mendip scenery. The course of ancient

streams have created vast subterran-ean caverns in the porous rock. Where these roofs have collapsed open gorges have been formed of which there are fine examples at Cheddar and Ebbor.

To the south the Mendip Hills present a steep front rising abruptly from the plains. The terrain to the north is inherent of glacial tundra with rolling hillocks that, when viewed from a vantage point on the hilltops, appear as a turbulent sea of verdant patchwork.

From Axbridge follow the A38 that carves a path north through a breach in the hills. The wooded slopes and scattered villages clinging to the limestone outcrops provide welcome interest after the flat lands of the previous day. Continue through the villages of Winscombe, Churchill and Lower Langford until once again the terrain levels as the route begins the run into Bristol.

Bristol   **16.1 miles/31 miles**   **(200.6 miles)**

Campsite: $^1/_2$m W of Bristol centre A370; Youth Hostel, B&B, Guest Houses, Hotels.

Tourist Information, Post Office, Rail Station, Hospital, Theatres, Cinemas, Banks, Library, Cycle Shop, Shops.

Bristol has a strong maritime history. The city itself grew up around the harbour at the mouth of the Avon and rapidly established itself as an important trade centre for export. The city has historic connections with the discovery of America since many of the early settlers sailed from the port. The Avon Gorge is spanned by Brunel's famous suspension bridge.

The course taken through the city is largely a matter of preference dependent on what attractions the city holds. For some it will merely provide an unwelcome obstacle to be overcome as quickly as possible while for others it will be a place of interest at which to spend some time.

The quickest way through the city is to follow the A38 into the city centre from where an inner ring road gives access to the desired escape route. Although quick, this route is not overly pleasant and demands a determined approach for the most satisfactory result.

An alternative follows the bank of the Avon to the west of the city before continuing north on the A38 to Stroud as follows:

Follow the A38 to reach Bridgwater Road. This leads to Bedminster Down Road and delivers a nervous cyclist at a large roundabout named "The Batches". Turn left to follow the A3029 that leads over a further roundabout to Brunel Way. This crosses the entrance to the floating harbour, then makes a left turn to join Hotwell Road on the banks of the Avon, with the Clifton Suspension Bridge spanning the Avon Gorge ahead. Join the cycleway beside the road and follow it in the direction of Avonmouth. After nearly 3 miles reach the area of Sea Mills and turn right by a golf course on the A4162 onto Sylvan Way. Continue along Dingle Road, Canford Lane and Canford Road before turning left on the A4018 to climb Brentry Hill and continue to the intersection with junction 16 of the M5, first along Passage Road, then Wyck Beck and finally The Causeway. The B4055 now leads pleasantly to the town of Almondsbury where the A38 is rejoined at a very convenient village corner shop.

The Cotswolds

The Cotswolds is an area of unforgettable natural beauty formed by a band of limestone rock that stretches north-east to the Humber and south-west to the Blackdown Hills. The exposed western edge of this rock band commands a fine viewpoint across the Severn to the hills of South Wales and it is this edge that provides the most imposing scenery. The highest point is near Cheltenham at Cleeve Hill. This rises to just over 1000ft. It is the rock itself that characterises the area due to its extensive use as a building material. It can be found in the stone walls, bridges, cottages and churches and harmonises perfectly with the landscape.

Continue north on the A38 to contour the west flank of Stinchcombe Hill, passing through the villages of Alveston, Falfield, Stone, Woodford and Newport along a fast and furious road to turn right on the B4066 just after crossing a rail line signposted "Dursley". Follow this to a T-junction and turn left to another T-junction with the A4135. Turn right into Dursley (cycle shop), turning left just past the church on the B4066. The quiet road weaves pleasantly along the steep sided river valley before climbing through the wooded slopes past the village of Uley. The route continues along an undulating crest with beautiful views across the Cotswolds. The road passes Woodchester Park on the right before fringing the birch and oak trees of Stanley Wood. A series of short, heart-stopping descents leads down into the Frome Valley and the town of Stroud.

Stroud	**34.4 miles/65.4 miles**	**(235 miles)**

Campsite: 1¹/2m S off A46, 1m S on Rodborough Common; Youth Hostel, B&B, Hotel.
Tourist Information, Rail Station, Hospital, Post Office, Theatre, Cinema, Banks, Library, Shops.
Situated on the edge of the Cotswolds this bustling market town provides a scenic stopover after a long day in the saddle. The textile industry dates back to the 16th century and reached a peak in the early 19th century following the introduction of mechanised looms. St Lawrence church and the town hall are examples of the town's former wealth.

The alternative route visits the spectacular gorge at Cheddar before turning south-east along the A371 through the village of Wookey, famous for the cave system formed by the River Axe, and on to Wells.

Wells is Britain's smallest city with, perhaps, its most magnificent cathedral and is recommended as a variation to the route if time permits

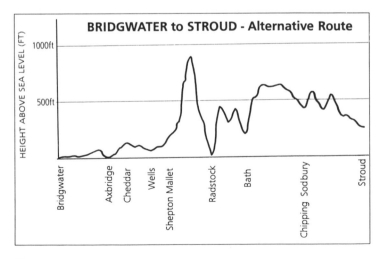

This city has one of the most magnificent cathedrals in England dating back to the 12th century.

The hills of Mendip still bar northward progress and the A371 provides the escape route into Shepton Mallet before finally turning north to join the A37 at Downside and continuing on the A367 to Radstock and on to Bath.

The preserved Roman spa with its impressive Victorian facade combines with the splendid Georgian architecture to make Bath one of the most elegant cities in the country.

Leave the city on London Road to join the A4 before once again turning north on the A46 that leads into the heart of the Cotswolds and on to Stroud. This route covers a distance of 57.5 miles, giving a total distance for the day of 72.4 miles. It would take approximately 6 hours' cycling time, which would obviously leave very little time for sightseeing, but if time allows the trip could be made over 2 days and is certainly recommended. Both Bath and Wells have cycle shops, and accommodation is available at all towns.

DAY 5: STROUD to IRONBRIDGE

Total Distance: **74.3 miles**
Cycling Time: **5 hours 55 minutes**

An initial ascent through the last of the upland Cotswolds leads to the regency spa town of Cheltenham and provides the warm-up for a day before continuing north along the course of the River Severn, the longest river in England and Wales. The Severn Valley carves a path northwards with Brendon Hill marking the head of the Vale of Evesham, famous for its crop of fruit. The town of Tewksbury nestles beneath the hill at the junction of the rivers Severn and Avon, with the Malvern Hills rising above the rolling patchwork of fields in the west. The cycling is easy once the Cotswolds have been overcome and follows a gentle course that always manages to maintain interest. The impressive cathedral of Worcester stands over the lush dairy pastures that surround it in an idyllic setting. The city's royal connections have always been strong and the area provided the stage for some decisive

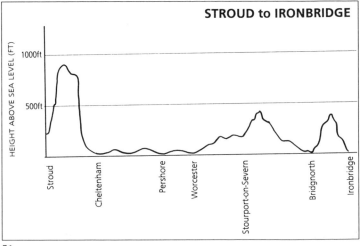

acts in the English civil war. The route enters the Wye Forest - a picturesque scrub of birch and oak, and continues along the course of the Severn Valley Railway that operates between Bewdley and Bridgnorth. Outcrops of the characteristic red sandstone can be seen all the way along this section and is much in evidence as a traditional building material. The day finishes at the centre of the 18th-century iron industry, and the catalyst that fired the Industrial Revolution. The Ironbridge Gorge provides a dramatic climax to another memorable day.

| **Stroud** | **0 miles** | **(235 miles)** |

Leave the town on the A46 along the Painswick Valley to reach the small town of Painswick. The road continues along the wooded ridge that forms the backbone of the Cotswold Way, a popular long distance walking route from Bath to Chipping Campden. The route is endowed with many viewpoints across the wooded Cotswold Hills that appear crisp and vivid in the light of the early morning sun, making this a delightful section to cycle.

A descent leads into Brockworth and a temporary departure from the hills before continuing straight over the roundabout to lead more easily through Shurdington and on into the spa town of Cheltenham.

A substitute to the above itinerary would be to leave Stroud by the B4070 and follow this through glorious countryside to the A417. A mile further down the road the B4070 continues north past Crickley Hill Country Park and the Devil's Chimney on the Cotswold Way into Cheltenham. The route is only about 3 miles longer and the cycling is slightly more challenging but it is an ideal route by which to enjoy the Cotswolds and could be used in conjunction with the main route from either Stroud or Cheltenham to form a short day excursion.

| **Cheltenham** | **12.4 miles** | **(247.4 miles)** |

Camping: 3m W off A40, 2m W off A40, 1¹/₂m NE on A436, 4m N off A435; B&B, Hotel.
Tourist Information, Rail Station, Hospital, Post Office, Bank, Theatre, Cinema, Library, Cycle Shop, Shops.
The spa town of Cheltenham is famed for its music and literature festivals

and, as one would expect from a town favoured by the gentry and nobility, boasts fine examples of Regency architecture overlooking tree-lined avenues and gardens. The town is a popular centre for exploring the Cotswolds.

From the centre of Cheltenham leave the town north on the A435 passing the famous racecourse on the right. Continue to the town of Bishop's Cleeve (camping available) with beautiful views back to the steep ridge that marks the western edge of the Cotswold escarpment. The road touches the outskirts of the town with Cleeve Hill and Nottingham Hill rising grandly in the east. Swift progress may now be made along the flat flood plain of the River Severn. The River Severn is the longest in Britain, flowing over 200 miles from its source in the heart of the Welsh Hills. Its course was diverted during the last Ice Age to its present one into the Bristol Channel estuary.

The road passes the isolated knoll of Oxenton Hill where a left fork is taken on the B4079. Continue easily to Aston Cross and Bredon where a right turn maintains northern progress on the B4080. The road passes the village of Bredon's Norton, nestled beneath the ramparts of the Bredon Hills which have been themselves an important settlement since the Bronze Age. The Malvern Hills form an impressive backdrop to the west.

Continue first to Eckington and then by the A4104 to Pershore (cycle shop) situated on the River Avon. The B4082 leads north from the river basin to pass Pershore station along the course of Piddle Brook, a tributary of the Avon. A left turn immediately after the station follows a delightfully varied course through glorious open countryside to the A422 which leads left into Worcester.

Worcester city centre can be avoided if so desired by following the A4538 first to Tibberton at junction 6 on the M5 and then to Martin Hussingtree when the A38 leads to the west of Droitwich to a junction with the A4133. This continues west to cross the A449 at Ombersley and rejoins the route at Holt Heath on the west bank of the Severn. The total distance from the A4538 to Holt Heath is 10 miles.

Worcester   26.1 miles/38.5 miles   (273.5 miles)

Camping: 2m S off A38, ¹/₂m NW off A449, 3¹/₂m on A449; B&B, Hotel. Tourist Information, Rail Station, Hospital, Post Office, Bank, Theatre, Cinema, Library, Cycle Shop, Shops.

The centrepiece of this medieval city is the imposing cathedral built on the banks of the River Severn between the 11th and 14th centuries on the site of an earlier monastery. It is the burial site of King John who ruled England in the 13th century. The city is also recognised for its porcelain industry and more recently for its sauce.

From the centre of Worcester cross the river and follow its right bank north. A short climb leads through the suburbs of the city to reach the village of Hallow after about 2 miles. The landscape has undergone a subtle change with the river now carving deep courses into the underlying red sandstone. The area betrays an inheritance from the Ice Age

*The city of Worcester with its 11th century cathedral reflected
in the waters of the River Severn*

with its distinctive rolling hills formed at the head of the great ice sheet that covered the land in approximately 10,000 BC.

It is a delight to cycle, with an ever changing panorama of wooded slopes, narrow overhung lanes, twisting roads and ancient woodlands.

From Holt Heath the B4196 runs parallel to the River Severn, winding through small villages to pass Shrawley Wood before crossing the Dick Brook. At the fork in the road turn right to descend into Stourport-on-Severn (cycle shop).

Stourport-on-Severn

Stourport grew from a small village into a major inland port in the mid 18th century due to the construction of the canal linking the Severn and the Trent. This industrial inheritance is still much in evidence.

A route avoiding Stourport-on-Severn would be to continue along the B4194 before descending to the right bank of the river into the south-west peninsula of the Wyre Forest into Bewdley.

Bewdley   **14.3 miles/52.8 miles**   **(287.8 miles)**

Campsite: 4m W on A456/A4117, ¹/₂m W of Stourport on Lickhill Road, B&B, Hotel.
Tourist Information, Post Office, Bank, Library, Shops.
Situated on the south-east fringe of the Wyre Forest, Bewdley clings to the steep sided banks of the River Severn. A three-arched bridge designed by Thomas Telford spans the river and the town is the southern terminus of the Severn Valley Railway that attracts thousands of steam enthusiasts each year.

The road continues from the crossroads by the church in the centre of Bewdley through the Wyre Forest to reach the village of Kinlet. From here join the B4555 and continue into Highley. A high ridge now leads between two deep river valleys to Chelmarsh where the road turns east before shadowing the course of the Severn Valley Railway into Bridgnorth.

Bridgnorth   **14.5 miles/67.3 miles**   **(302.3 miles)**

Campsite: 2m E on A458; B&B, Hotel.
Tourist Information, Post Office, Bank, Theatre, Cinema, Library, Cycle Shop, Shops.
The centrepiece of the town is a six-arch bridge that crosses the River Severn. The town itself is a beautiful collection of timber-framed houses nestled between the numerous sandstone outcrops. Bridgnorth is the starting point for the Severn Valley Railway. The whistle of steam echoes around the valley every weekend of the year as enthusiasts and tourists alike enjoy the trip south to Bewdley along the course of the river valley. The high town is built on the cliffs overlooking the river and is reached either by winding roads, steps and back alleys or by the steepest cliff railway in England. The teetering remains of the Norman keep make the famous tower at Pisa appear perfectly straight, and the area commands lovely views across the river to the medieval town huddled against the far river bank.

Leave Bridgnorth on the A442 to navigate a tree-lined route

Bridgnorth is one of the most attractive towns in Shropshire

dotted with outcrops of ochre rock. Cross the narrow bridge spanning the River Worfe to reach a roundabout where a left turn leads to a campsite after a few miles on the left.

Ironbridge   7 miles/74.3 miles   (309.3 miles)

Campsite: 3m S of Telford on A442; Youth Hostel, B&B, Guest House, Hotel.

Tourist Information, Rail Station, Banks, Cycle Shop (Telford), Shops.

North-east of the Shropshire hills in the shadow of the Wrenkin seems an unlikely setting for a revolution. However, it was here in the 18th century that the use of coke was first employed to smelt iron ore and the first steam engine was built to run on rails. A discovery of equivalent significance today would be to design a car that could run on water instead of petrol! The town of Ironbridge now exhibits only a remnant of its former prosperity. The town clings to the steep banks of the gorge overlooked by the iron bridge that symbolises its assured place in the history books.

The new town of Telford has grown up of recent years around a complex design of dual carriageway and roundabouts that probably look more aesthetic on the planners' drawing board than on the Shropshire countryside. The town has yet to live up to its title as the "Forest city".

DAY 6: IRONBRIDGE to WARRINGTON

Total Distance: **62.4 miles**
Cycling Time: **4 hours 40 minutes**

The county of Shropshire is bordered by the Welsh hills to the west and the Pennines to the east and provides the route north. The town of Whitchurch on the Welsh border leads into Cheshire, an area that was once a Roman stronghold. Chester is the centrepiece of the county and is the finest example of an English walled city in the country with exquisite displays of black and white Tudor houses in galleried arcades along the main street. The day's cycling is not strenuous, taking a tranquil line through the rich rolling farmlands to reach the Delamere Forest to the east of the industrialised Wirral Peninsula. The variety of red sandstone available as local building material has been very influential in shaping the appearance of the area. The landscape gently rises and falls over the whalebacked mounds of buried rock that occasionally pierce the grassy veneer to form rugged outcrops. The route ends on the edge of the industrial north and the town of Warrington.

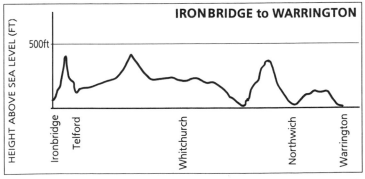

Ironbridge provides a potent symbol of the Industrial Revolution that was to change the world

Ironbridge/Telford   0 miles (309.3 miles)

There are many variations of route that lead through the urban sprawl that has built up around the banks of the Severn.

From the cyclists' point of view, unless there is a specific reason for exploring the area, it would be advantageous to make an early start and use the dual carriageway that carves a north/south path through the metropolis to join the A442 on the northern outskirts of Telford. From here the road passes easily

64

through open countryside to Crudgington. After the village stores on the right, continue to Waters Upton where a long climb of almost 2 miles begins before levelling along an

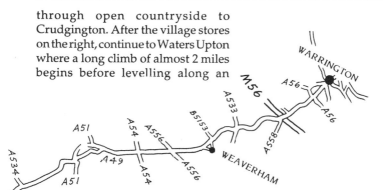

avenue of rhododendrons. Two sharp bends lead to a junction in the village of Hodnet where the A442 leads left at the brow of a short hill.

Pass by a church on an undulating road lined with more rhododendrons and take a sharp right by a distinctive timber-framed cottage. A descent and a series of bends deliver the cyclist into open countryside once more where a long straight finally reaches the junction with the A41. A left turn then delivers the cyclist easily into Whitchurch.

Whitchurch   28.9 miles   (338.2 miles)

Campsite: 1m N on A41, 4$^{1}/_{2}$m SE off A41 / A442; B&B, Hotel.
Tourist Information, Rail Station, Post Office, Bank, Cycle Shop, Shops.
Whitchurch is a small market town on the Welsh/Cheshire border.

From the town centre follow signs to Warrington (A49) over a series of roundabouts to pass Hinton Hall before entering the county of Cheshire. Pass a waterfowl sanctuary on the right before crossing the Shropshire Union Canal from where the road continues through scenic meadowland to pass the impressive entrance to Cholmondeley Castle on the left. Pass through the pretty villages of Ridley Green, Spurstow and Bunbury Heath to reach the mound of Beeston Castle on the left. The route enters Tiverton where a short climb leads to a set of traffic lights. Follow signs into the village of Tarporley, ignoring the newly constructed bypass that circumnavigates the village, and rejoin the A49 with spectacular views across the Gowy Valley. Descend into Cotebrook before climbing once more to reach a junction with the A54. Continue on the A49 to cross a railway line and skirt the town of Weaverham about 2 miles west of Northwich.

Northwich   22.3 miles/51.2 miles   (360.5 miles)

Campsite: 4m NW on A49, 4m SW off A556, 2m W on bank of Trent and Mersey Canal; B&B, Hotel.
Tourist Information, Rail Station, Hospital, Post Office, Bank, Cinema, Library, Cycle Shop, Shops.
Northwich is famous for the rock salt beds it is built on. Salt has been mined here since Roman times and is still extracted today. The unique Anderton lift links the River Weaver with the Trent and Mersey Canal.

Continue on the A49 to cross the Trent and Mersey Canal and the junction with the A533. The villages of Lower Whitley and Higher Whitley depict the perfect image of rural England that is immediately shattered as the road crosses the M56 motorway. Continue into Warrington, crossing the Manchester Ship Canal to reach the town centre.

Warrington   11.2 miles/62.4 miles   (371.7 miles)

Campsite: 5¹/₂m E off A57 (J21 on M6); B&B, Hotel.
Tourist Information, Rail Station, Hospital, Post Office, Bank, Cinema, Library, Cycle Shop, Shops.
Warrington is situated at the head of the Mersey and is renowned for the beer industry that has grown to produce more beer than the traditional breweries at Burton-on-Trent. A statue of Cromwell stands near the bridge to commemorate his victory over the Royalist forces in 1648 at Preston.

DAY 7: WARRINGTON to KIRKBY LONSDALE

Total Distance: 63.8 miles (70.1 miles using the Lancs. Cycle Way)

Cycling time: 5 hours 15 minutes (6 hours)

An industrialised barricade stretches across the country from Liverpool in the west to Humberside in the east, presenting a seemingly impenetrable band of urban sprawl to the northbound cyclist. The counties of Merseyside and Greater Manchester segregate the open countryside of Cheshire in the south and Lancashire in the north. This, on the face of it, seems no place for the cyclist but the truth is rather different. Liverpool grew as a port in the early 18th century, extracting its wealth from the trade of sugar and slaves. Its prosperity continued through the Industrial Revolution where it provided an outlet for textiles that were being produced in the newly created city of Manchester. The construction of the Manchester Ship Canal is a

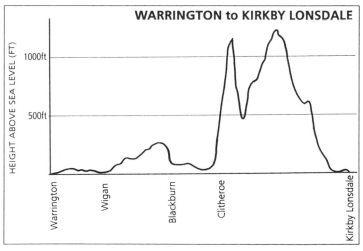

stunning example of the wealth, power and ambition that was inherent of the Victorian age. The canal opened in 1894 and provided the city with independent access to the Mersey and the valuable export markets.

The cycle route weaves through the many backroads and wealthy suburban villages that remain surprisingly untouched by the proximity of the large industrial centres. Progress north is aided by use of the Lancashire cycleways. Lancashire council have provided two cycleways, each of approximately 130 miles in length, touring the south and north of the county. The southern route can be picked up north of Chorley and followed to Whalley from where the northern route continues to Kirkby Lonsdale. The Lancastrian town of Blackburn borders the Forest of Bowland and signals the passing into more rural terrain. The route continues through the forest on a contrasting course of steep ascents and wide open space to the Lune Valley in the heart of the Lancashire moors and the town of Kirkby Lonsdale.

| **Warrington** | **0 miles** | **(371.7 miles)** |

The A49 provides the initial lifeline out of Warrington and leads via a series of roundabouts and dual carriageway to a junction with the M62. Another short section leads after a few hundred yards to a further junction which is followed first left (A49 Newton-le-Willows) and then right to continue through Winwick

on the A573. Pass through Hermitage Green to cross the M6 motorway and arrive at Golborne after a hair-raising crossing of the A580. Cross the Leeds and Liverpool Canal to reach Platt Bridge where a left turn is followed into the centre of Wigan.

Wigan 11.3 miles
(383 miles)

B&B, Guest houses, Hotel. Tourist Information, Rail Station, Hospital, Post Office, Bank, Library, Theatre, Cinema, Cycle Shop, Shops.

Wigan's history dates from Roman times when it was established as a stronghold to keep the marauding Scots and Picts at bay. Coal has been mined in the area since the 14th century but real prosperity did not reach the town until the 18th century following the construction of the Leeds and Liverpool Canal. The loading point for the coal was at the now famous Wigan Pier.

Pass under the rail line and cross the A577 to reach a dual carriageway. Turn right at the end of the street and right again, followed by a left turn at a roundabout. Continue alongside a river before crossing it signposted "Standish". Pass the royal infirmary on the left and continue along parades of shops. Cross the railway line before immediately turning right on the A5106 to recross it on the road to Chorley. The concrete and brick begins to recede and give way to more open countryside and a few miles of mental relaxation.

At a junction with the A6 turn left and continue into Chorley (cycle shops). The A6 leads out of the town crossing the railway line by a short section of dual carriageway that continues to junction 8 with the M61. From this point there is a choice of routes, each tracing a path north-east into the Ribble Valley, the Forest of Bowland and the North Yorkshire Moors.

The first follows a more direct course and is recommended if time or weather conditions are not especially favourable. The route is 63.8 miles and will take approximately 5 hours 15 minutes' cycling time to reach the scheduled overnight stop at Kirkby Lonsdale.

The other follows the northern section of the Lancashire Cycle Way. The cycle track was established by the county council in consultation with Friends of the Earth and was opened in 1982. It has been designed to guide the visitor through a network of minor roads that avoids the large urbanised areas and best displays the many areas of outstanding beauty that the county has to offer. The route is recommended if time allows. Full details of the Lancashire Cycle Way and other cycling routes in the county can be obtained at any tourist information centre or direct from Lancashire County Planning Office at the County Offices in Preston. The cycle route is waymarked throughout.

The alternative and more direct route follows the A674 across the motorway and the Leeds and Liverpool Canal to continue through the villages of Wheelton and Higher Wheelton. Continue straight over the roundabout and recross the canal before joining the A6061 that leads into Blackburn.

Blackburn   **17.2 miles/28.5 miles**   **(400.2 miles)**

B&B, Guest Houses, Hotel
Tourist Information, Rail Station, Hospital, Post Office, Bank, Library, Cinema, Cycle Shop, Shops.
Blackburn provides the last stopping point for travellers before crossing the moors to the north. The moors form a natural barrier and it was for this reason that Blackburn grew up as an important staging post. The Lewis Textile Museum in the town illustrates the more recent history and the turbulent times that surrounded the introduction of mechanisation into the area's traditional textile industry.

The strong of heart may simply head for the town centre from which the A666 leads to Clitheroe (16.7 miles) but a more pleasant path stays on the A674 to pass the rail station and cross the canal from where a left turn follows the B6447 on the fringe of Wilton Country

Park. Follow straight ahead as the road bears round to the right and reach a crossroads with the A677. Pass this and continue with good views left across the Ribble Valley to meet the B6233. This joins the A6119 which is followed right to a roundabout. The A666 then maintains progress through Wilpshire and Langho and under a rail bridge to a large roundabout where the A59 is taken to the A671 which is then followed left into Clitheroe.

The alternative course avoids Blackburn and picks up the Lancashire Cycle Way at Whittle-le-Woods 1¹/₂ miles north on the A6 from junction 8. Take the first turning right after the B6229 and turn right at the T-junction to pass under the M61 motorway and over the Leeds and Liverpool Canal. From this point the cyclist is guided by the cycle route waymarks across country to the villages of Lower Copthurst and Brindle on the B5256 and via the A675 to Hoghton and on to Samlesbury Bottoms and Mellor after crossing the A677. Top of Ramsgreave is the next village before crossing the A666 and continuing to Whalley via York and Hollinhall. The route continues on the B6246 beneath the viaduct to descend into the Ribble Valley to cross the river at Great Mitton. Cross the junction with the B6243 and turn right at the crossroads to Waddington through Bashall town. The B6478 can now be followed right into Clitheroe or the cycle route can be followed through Waddington and on to Slaidburn (see below).

Clitheroe	**11.1 miles/39.6 miles**	**(411.3 miles)**

Tourist Information, Cycle Shop, Shops.
The town is nestled in the Ribble Valley between the Forest of Bowland and Pendle Hill - a rumoured meeting place for witches. The main street winds up to Clitheroe Castle, a Norman construction perched on an outcrop of limestone rock.

Two routes can now be taken into Slaidburn:

1) The cycle track chooses a course from Waddington around Easington Fell and through West Bradford and Grindleton to Slaidburn (9.7 miles).

2) The direct route and probably the most satisfying climbs the 350 metres over Easington Fell. The view from the pass on a clear day is very rewarding with the town of Clitheroe in the south huddled beneath the slopes of Pendle Hill, and the picturesque river valleys carving paths through the beautiful Forest of Bowland.

The descent from the pass is steep and exhilarating which heightens awareness to fact that the area is quite remote and help could be a long time reaching an injured cyclist. The road crosses the River Hodder and turns right to skirt Dunbow Hill before descending steeply once more into Slaidburn (6.2 miles).

Forest of Bowland
This area of open moorland has survived the passing of the Industrial Revolution to remain an area of natural wilderness. After the Norman invasion the forest was declared a hunting ground and through the ages has provided refuge for many fugitives. The trees have disappeared leaving a desolate area of open grazing for hardy sheep and cattle. It is quite possible to cross this 15-mile stretch without sight of another person and due to its altitude and notorious spells of bad weather it is also possible to cross the area without sight of your front wheel!

From the war memorial the Lancashire Cycle Way may once more be followed out across the open moorland. This 12-mile section is as remote as any encountered. The climbs initially appear unending with a final demoralising sting before reaching a cattle grid. The gradient finally relents to allow the beauty of the area to be fully appreciated. From the second cattle grid a solitary road can be seen climbing into the distance along the side of the fell. The road rises first to cross Lythe Fell and then again over Tatham Fell before a final descent leads into North Yorkshire and the town of High Bentham and a welcome breather. Follow the B6480 left through Low Bentham and back into Lancashire and along the course of the River Wenning and the railway. Before reaching Wennington turn right (cycleway) to Wrayton to join the A683. Turn right and cross the river and turn left into Tunstall and Burrow. Join the A65 and turn left into Kirkby Lonsdale.

Kirkby Lonsdale   24.2 miles/63.8 miles   (435.5 miles)

Campsite: ¹/₂m SE off A65; B&B, Hotel.
Tourist Information, Post Office, Bank, Shops.
A picturesque English village situated on the River Lune in the river valley between the North York Moors and the Cumbrian mountains. The old market square is one of the many delightful features in this historic town. Shops offer all facilities to the saddle-weary traveller. The Devil's Bridge that spans the river is a beautiful site and popular with visitors to the area.

DAY 8: KIRKBY LONSDALE to GRETNA

Total Distance:	88.7 miles
Cycling time:	6 hours 50 minutes

The day's itinerary follows the eastern leg of the Cumbrian Cycle Way that traces the Eden Valley north-east between the Pennines and the Cumbrian mountains. The route was established in order to make available the lesser known areas of Cumbria. The entire circuit is 259 miles and can be completed in 7 days at an average of 37 miles' cycling per day. The route is well waymarked throughout by the standard highways cycle route marker. Little used minor roads guide the cyclist gently through countryside that is often ignored by regular visitors to the area. It is almost impossible to lose direction but care is always required at each junction to avoid frustrating deviations. The mileage for the day is high but despite this the cycling is never

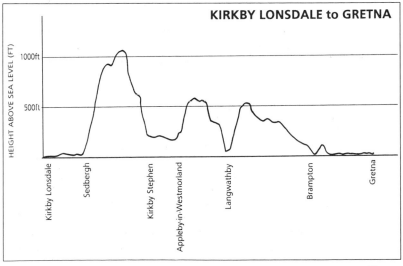

difficult and for those attempting the full distance a steady pace will pay dividends.

The route accompanies the River Lune to the small market town of Sedbergh from where a steep climb leads into the remote valley at Mallerstang and the source of the River Eden. Again the river is followed north through a patchwork of grazing meadows that carpet the widening valley floor. The hills of the North Yorkshire Moors begin to retreat as the Lune merges into the estuary of the Solway Firth at the fortress town of Carlisle. The border has always held a great significance through history and has been the site of many conflicts. Emperor Hadrian constructed the famous wall in AD 122 which runs the width of the country as a deterrent to the tribes of the north. The border crossing on this tour has also a great significance as the cyclist leaves England and brings the goal of John O'Groats that much closer.

The Yorkshire Dales

The area shares little of the geological history of the neighbouring Lake District and was formed by a succession of upheavals in the earth's crust. Violent faults tore the underlying limestones, thrusting the rock to the surface, forming outcrops and escarpments. Millions of years of erosion by the elements and successive Ice Ages has altered the area to be finally shaped by the hand of man into the present day expanse of high moorland upland. Traditional karste features dominate the natural landscape of weathered limestone and there is a proliferation of deep gorges, waterfalls and underground caves and caverns linked by complex networks of streams.

The area has traditionally been farmed, an activity that has ultimately sculpted the present landscape of drystone wall and rustic homesteads. The area did not survive the Industrial Revolution completely unscathed and the mining of lead and quarrying of limestone as building materials have left their scars.

The area was designated a National Park in 1954 and is now enjoyed by many visitors each year. It is largely overshadowed in popularity by the Cumbrian mountains but in many ways this fact only serves to enhance its beauty and maintain its sanctity as an unspoilt rural corner of Britain.

CROSS FELL

Kirkby Lonsdale — 0 miles (435.5 miles)

If time is short or the weather unfavourable the direct route from

MURTON FELL

DUFTON

APPLEBY-IN-WESTMORLAND

A66

B6412

A66

A685

KIRKBY STEPHEN

A685

B6259

WILD BOAR FELL

A684

A683

A684

SEDBERGH

GARSDALE

Kirkby Lonsdale is via the A683 and is recommended. The road mimics the course of the Lune along an old Roman road and is generally easy cycling.

The alternative is to use the cycleway that selects quieter backroads on the west side of the river (9.6 miles). From the centre of Kirkby Lonsdale follow the B6254 past the church until a right turn is signposted at Kearstwick. The road follows the river basin past Scar Brow, Mansergh Hall and Nether Hall before a sharp climb leads away from the river and a delightful balcony section. A right turn is taken at the bottom of another hill to

A683

A65

KIRKBY LONSDALE

Rigmaden Farm through Rigmaden Park and over the Lune to join the A683 to Middleton. The main road is then followed directly into Sedbergh (10.9 miles).

Sedbergh   **9.6 miles**   **(445.1 miles)**

Campsite: 6m SE off A684, 2m W on A684, $^1/_2$m E on Hawes road; Youth Hostel at Stonehouse, B&B.

Tourist Information (Yorkshire Dales National Parks Information Centre), Mountain Rescue Post, Post Office, Shops.

The town lies at the junction of five valleys and is a focal point for visitors to the region. It provides an excellent centre to explore the surrounding fells.

The A684 leads east and crosses the River Rawthey at the far side of the town and commences the slow climb through Garsdale to reach the Moorcock Inn and the junction with the B6259. Garsdale is sandwiched dramatically between the peaks of Baugh Fell and Rise Hill and its scenery is possibly the most captivating on the trip. The B6259 leads north following the line of the railway and at the boundary of the National Park passes the waterfall that spawns the River Eden. The river begins to widen, fed by the streams from Wild Boar Fell, Mallerstang Edge and Little Fell. The 12th-century Pendragon Castle stands by the roadside and is reputed to have been the home of Uther Pendragon, the father of King Arthur. The route continues easily to the village of Nateby and finally on to Kirkby Stephen.

Kirkby Stephen   **20.2 miles/29.8 miles**   **(465.3 miles)**

Campsite: $^1/_4$m S off A685; Youth Hostel, B&B.

Tourist Information, Rail Station, Post Office, Cycle Shop, Shops.

This small town is superbly situated in high mountain scenery with views as memorable as the cathedral-styled church in the town centre.

The route now leaves the main road to cross the undulating hillocks that dominate the western fringe of the Pennines. Turn left opposite the church to pass the school and continue to Soulby. Two steep climbs deliver weary legs to nearly 700ft before a long welcome descent leads after a few miles to the B6260 and Appleby-in-Westmorland.

Appleby-in-Westmorland   10.6 miles/40.4 miles   (475.9 miles)

Campsite: 2m S off B6260, 2m SSE off B6260; B&B, Youth Hostel at Dufton.

Tourist Information, Rail Station, Hospital, Post Office, Bank, Library, Cycle Shop, Shops.

Appleby-in-Westmorland is the main tourist centre for visitors who wish to acquaint themselves with the footpaths and country lanes of the northern Pennines and the Eden Valley. The market town was allocated as the county town after the Norman conquest and grew up around a Norman stronghold that valued the strategic position at the head of the Eden Valley. The castle now has a large collection of wild birds and rare farm animals and has been established as the Appleby Castle Conservation Centre. The town hosts the largest horse fair in Britain each June.

The cycle track now traces an intricate path in the widening Eden Valley beneath the Pennine scarp and the tops of Murton and Dufton Fells and Mibune Forest. The area is a favourite for walking and the Pennine Way visits the village of Dufton where there is a youth hostel. The cycleway continues to Knock, Milburn and Blencarn followed by a testing climb to Kirkland before veering west to Skirwith and Langwathby.

From Langwathby the B6413 may be taken although there is no advantage in distance over the cycleway as long as care is exercised with the route-finding at each junction.

Long Meg and her daughters, between Little Salkeld and Glassonby, dates from Neolithic times and is the second largest stone circle in England.

The B6413 joins the cycle track just before a steep descent to cross the Croglin Water. A climb leads to easier ground and a pleasant section through Newbiggin, Castle Carrock and on to Brampton.

Brampton   33.5 miles/73.9 miles   (509.4 miles)

Campsite: ¹/2m N off A6071; Youth Hostel at Greenhead 8m E on A69, B&B.

Tourist Information, Rail Station.

This charming cobbled town has changed little in character over the last century. The buildings are made predominantly of local sandstone and the parish church was constructed by the Normans using stone from nearby Hadrian's Wall. The wall is within easy reach and a fine view may be gained from just outside the town at Banks. This fortified line that crosses the

73½ *mile width of the country from Wallsend to the Solway Firth was completed in AD 122-126. Turrets were placed along its length and were manned by garrisons from 16 strategically sited forts. The Written Rock bears an inscription by one such soldier posted to this remote Roman outpost.*

The beautiful Talkin Tarn is also worth a visit, situated to the south of the town within the country park that bears its name.

The final 15 miles to Gretna are relatively painless. The glacial "Kames" that form the hillocked landscape around Brampton is left behind as the route crosses the estuary of the Esk and the Eden. Follow the A6071, passing through Smithfield to reach Longtown on the River Esk. The road continues easily across the border into Scotland to reach the town of Gretna and a significant milestone on the journey.

Gretna   **14.8 miles/88.7 miles**   **(524 2 miles)**

Campsite: ¼m W on B721, 3m NW off A74, ¼m E off A74; B&B.
Situated at the head of the Solway Firth, Gretna is known throughout the British Isles for the smithy and blacksmiths' shop where runaway couples could be married. Legislation of 1940 put an end to the service but the romanticism that surrounds the area is very much alive.

The route explores the delights of the countryside presenting many unforgettable views

DAY 9: GRETNA to CUMNOCK

Total Distance: **73 miles**
Cycling Time: **5 hours 20 minutes**

The day's route crosses the border county of Dumfries and Galloway in the Scottish Lowlands. The area is often unjustly overlooked by visitors travelling north to the Highlands. The Solway Firth cuts deep into the mainland giving rise to an intricate coastline that is perhaps some of the most beautiful in Britain. The route from Gretna follows the coast road along heather-covered hills fringed by sandy inlets with views south to the Cumbrian mountains that are particularly stunning in the early morning or at sunset. The tidal saltmarsh between Ruthwell and Glencaple is administered by the Wildfowl Trust and is sanctuary to many species of wildfowl that visit in winter. The underlying red sandstone that predominates the region is nowhere more evident than the historic town of Dumfries where plentiful use has been made of the stone as a building material. From Dumfries the route joins the local KM Trail Cycleway established by the local authority to celebrate the invention of the first pedal powered bicycle by the local blacksmith Kirkpatrick Macmillan in 1839. This was the first rearwheel driven "velocipede" but sadly did not arouse much more than local curiosity and it was not until the advent of the

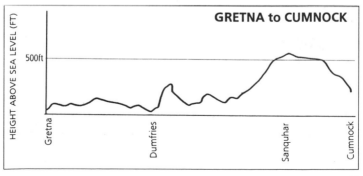

"safety bicycle" in 1884 that the rearwheel drive concept was accepted. Sadly Macmillan died in 1878 without realising the

breakthrough he had pioneered. The Nith Valley provides the setting for further northern progress, passing Drumlanrig Castle before reaching Sanquhar and the main A76 which is followed to Cumnock.

Gretna   0 miles   (524.2 miles)

From Gretna follow the B721 west to pass through a number of small hamlets to reach Eastriggs. The road continues through Dornock to cross the railway line before reaching Annan.

Annan   7.8 miles   (532 miles)

Campsite: ¹/2m N on B722; B&B, Hotel.
Rail Station, Post Office, Bank, Shops.
Small market town that was the site of a viaduct rail crossing into the Cumbrian coast. The Solway Firth is 1¹/2 miles wide at this point. The crossing was dismantled at the end of the 19th century after suffering severe storm damage.

Leave the town centre on the B723 to cross the River Annan and begin a slow climb. Turn left on the B724 signposted Cummertrees and continue more easily along this beautiful coastal section with views across the Solway Firth to the Cumbrian mountains. The road follows the course of the rail line to Dumfries, crossing it at

Cummertrees and again at Summerfield. At the next milestone beyond Summerfield turn left on the B725 and continue easily along the estuary to Bankend nestled beneath the Bankend Hill. Turn right and begin a steady climb with views across to the Mabie Forest to eventually arrive at the town of Dumfries.

Dumfries 17.4 miles/25.2 miles (549.4 miles)

Campsite: 1¹/₂m E on A780/A75; B&B, Hotels.
Tourist Information, Rail Station, Hospital, Post Office, Bank, Theatre, Cinema, Library, Cycle Shop, Shops.

Dumfries is the market centre for the Southern Lowlands but despite this pastoral facade, history has not passed the town by. Robert the Bruce declared independence over the English here in 1306. The poet Robert Burns died in the town and Bonnie Prince Charlie looted the church to fund his campaign against the English. The red sandstone buildings characterise the architecture and the old town hall in the market places dates from the early 18th century. A medieval stone bridge crosses the river before the Nith widens to fall over the semi-circular weirs that have become one of the attractions of the town for visitors.

From the tourist information centre the KM trail crosses the river and continues along College Street/College Road to cross the railway and main Dumfries ring road (A75). A left turn into Stewartry Road is followed by another left into Priory Avenue. Cross the A76 and continue into Lochside Road. Follow signs that lead to Newbridge via Newton Road and Irongray Road.

Descend to cross the Cluden Water and climb a short hill to pass the "12 Apostles" standing stones.

Continue along the B729 for approximately 6 miles to Dunscore and take the first turning right to climb a hill that leads through the narrow gap between Hillhead

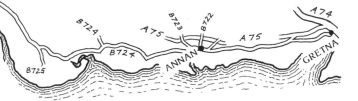

and Benan Hill to Glenmidge. Turn left from where a final short climb leads to the long gentle descent into Keir Mill. The terrain has become suddenly more dramatic with the Keir Hills dominating the western horizon and the evergreen plantation of the Forest of Ae creeping onto the lower slopes of the Lowther Hills in the east.

The blacksmiths where Macmillan worked is situated ½ mile past Keir Mill with a commemorative plaque on the gable end.

The route turns right by the telephone box in Keir Mill to pass the cemetery on the right where Macmillan was buried and cross the Scaur Water to reach a T-junction with the A702 after about a mile. Turn right and then left on a forest-fringed back lane that leads to Drumlanrig Castle. The approach is very impressive.

The castle was built in the 17th century as a stately home and is now open to the public. It also houses a cycle museum devoted to the history of two-wheeled transport.

A track should now be followed through Drumlanrig Park on a course high above the Nith Valley on the west bank. The road eventually descends to the west bank and follows the river before crossing it onto the A76 at Eilock Bridge. The A76 is then followed for 2 miles into Sanquhar.

Sanquhar   30.4 miles/55.6 miles   (579.8 miles)

B&B, Hotel.
Tourist Information, Post Office, Bank, Shops.

Sanquhar is an interesting town, not least for the name, situated in the upper Nith Valley beneath the Lowther Hills. The town was the site of an 18th-century toll gate for travellers on journeys north. Gold and lead account for the old disused mine workings in the hills that are now only occupied by sheep, grouse and hillwalkers. The Southern Upland Way passes through the town en route to Reed Point on the west coast, having started its journey at Dunskey Castle on the east coast.

The A76 continues along the Nith Valley with the Lowland hills dominating the views all around. Kirkland Hill rises steeply (1670ft) above the town of Kirkconnel to the north with the imposing Blackcraig Hill (2300ft) to the south. The route follows a steady course by the river and allows time to indulge in the natural splendour of the valley. If the weather is not too accommodating the town of New Cumnock provides a welcome break but apart from that it is not inspiring.

The A76 crosses Afton Water before turning north at a mini-roundabout to cross the Nith. The route now leaves the sanctuary of the Nith Valley and a more undulating course is followed to Cumnock.

Cumnock   **17.4 miles/73 miles**   **(597.2 miles)**

Campsite: 1/2m N on A76; B&B, Hotels.
Tourist Information, Post Office, Bank, Cinema, Cycle Shop, Shops.
Situated on the Lugar Water this pretty mining town has lost a great deal of its historic charm. The market cross is still in place and the municipal campsite is delightfully situated on the banks of the river.

DAY 10: CUMNOCK to ARDLUI

Total Distance:	**86.1 miles**
Cycling Time:	**6 hours**

The route endeavours to search out a course through the industrialised centres and suburbs clinging to the banks of the Clyde in the west and the Firth of Forth in the east. The choice largely depends on the selected route through the Grampian Mountains. The more direct would be to use the A9 trunk road to Inverness, but undoubtedly the most enjoyable is to follow the western coastline of Argyll to the highlands of Lochaber before crossing to Inverness along the most famous of Scottish lochs, Loch Ness. Glasgow can largely be avoided on the west side by use of the Erskine Bridge across the Clyde.

There has been extensive progress within Scotland to promote an expanding network of cycle paths. Sustrans was commissioned from 1983-85 to study the potential for cycle routes along abandoned railways, riversides and canal paths. The study revealed excellent opportunities and through co-ordination with local authorities, 150km of cycleway have been established. Many more are currently being proposed, not only in Scotland but across Britain.

The route follows the main road to Kilmarnock, from where a Sustrans route can be joined at the town of Kilwinning and followed

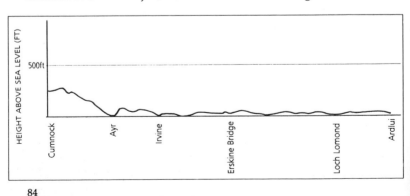

into the outskirts of Paisley where the road is rejoined for the crossing of the Clyde at Erskine. The Glasgow to Loch Lomond cycle route is then intercepted and leads delightfully from old Kilpatrick through Dumbarton and along the beautiful Vale of Leven to the banks of Loch Lomond. The western shore of the loch provides an unforgettable setting for the remainder of the ride to an overnight stop at Ardlui. The day is arduous mainly due to the mileage covered, although the cycling is nowhere too demanding. An early start is recommended and a steady progress through the day will again reap rewards.

The text gives general descriptions of the cycle route but full details are available in a series of single sheets containing route maps, descriptions and points of interest along the route from local tourist information offices or direct from the local council. Anybody wishing to find out more about the project will find the address for Sustrans under Additional Information.

Cumnock	**0 miles**	**(597.2 miles)**

Leave the centre of Cumnock on the B7083, passing the hospital on the right a little way out of town. Continue to cross the River Auchinleck before entering the town of the same name and pass under the rail bridge to a roundabout where the A76 is joined and followed pleasantly to the town of Mauchline. Continue along the main road, passing a rail line and a junction with the A719 before reaching another junction with the B7073. Turn left and follow this as the road fringes the suburbs of Kilmarnock and reaches Hurlford before finally joining the A71 at a roundabout. Continue straight ahead to Kilmarnock town centre.

Kilmarnock	**15.6 miles**	**612.8 miles**

Campsite: 4m NE on B769 at Dykehead; B&B.
Tourist Information, Rail Station, Bank, Post Office, Hospital, Cinema, Library, Cycle Shop, Shops.
The town is well known for the Johnnie Walker blend of whisky that has been bottled here since its discovery by a King Street grocer in 1820.

The area has more than its fair share of castles with Dean Castle being particularly beautiful. The Scottish poet Robert Burns is also commemorated in the town at Poets Tower in Kay Park, a spectacular Victorian structure over two storeys high.

Leave Kilmarnock on the main A735 to reach the town of Kilmaurs after about 2 miles. Cross the river and make a right turn followed by another past the post office by a church. The road leads under a rail bridge and continues to the village of Cunninghamhead at a junction with the B769. Continue straight ahead and cross the Annick Water to reach Torranyard at a junction with the A736. Cross this and in 2 miles reach the B785 in the village of Montgreenan. Turn right and continue into Kilwinning (10.5 miles/cycle shop).

To gain access to the cycle route turn right at the junction with the A737 and follow this to cross the River Garnock by Dalgarven Mill. Take the second turning on the right and follow this through houses for about 500yds and join the cycleway as it crosses the river.

Continue to Lochshore, a reclaimed recreation site with good picnic facilities, before leaving the disused rail line and continue along a beautiful country lane. Pass under the railway at the site of one of Scotland's oldest churches and follow the tree-lined lane as it climbs steadily to reach a junction with the B707 and A737 at Highfield.

The road continues along the crest of a ridge above the Garnock Valley to reach the B777 above the town of Kilbirnie. Turn right and immediately left at Longbar to follow the Art Trail, a permanent exhibition of environmental art, to join the cycle route once more before reaching the river. Pleasant progress can now be made over the next 8 1/2 miles before the rail line must once again be abandoned at Simple Town House and a short section of the A737 is followed into Paisley before a left turn is made at a roundabout on the A761.

The route to the Erskine Bridge is often busy and the road systems are generally quite "lively". After the serenity of the cycle route the busy road system is a bit of a shock but with a strong heart and a determined approach the route may be conquered.

Turn left on the A761 to rejoin the A737 signposted Erskine Bridge. This is followed to junction 29 of the M8 which thankfully diverts the majority of the traffic away from the A726 that leads relatively sedately to the bridge.

The Erskine Bridge was opened in 1971, is over 4000ft in length and designed to withstand winds of over 130mph.

Cross the bridge with splendid views along the River Clyde to join a cycle track that passes east under the span before crossing the railway line and the A814. A small bridge spans the Forth and Clyde Canal to join the cycleway on the towpath on the far side.

The Glasgow to Loch Lomond cycle route was completed in 1989 and covers 21 miles. The route runs parallel to the River Clyde utilising sections of disused rail lines before turning north along the towpath of the River Leven to follow the Leven Valley to Loch Lomond.

Turn right and continue under the Erskine Bridge to cross the main Dumbarton road into the Memorial Park at Bowling. The route is well signposted and leads easily into the Roman fortified town of Dumbarton.

Dumbarton   **36.8 miles/52.4 miles**   **(665.2 miles)**

B&B, Hotels.

Tourist Information, Rail Station, Hospital, Post Office, Bank, Theatre, Cinema, Library, Shops.

Situated on the River Leven and the Clyde the town has been of strategic importance to the Romans and then the Scots and has undergone a series of fortifications. Little remains today except the famous rock. Rapid growth of the town occurred in the 19th century due to the shipbuilding industry that was established here. The Cutty Sark *was built in Dumbarton in 1869.*

Enter Dumbarton along Crosslet Road, and continue to reach Dumbarton central station. Turn left under the railway and follow signs that lead across the River Leven at Bridge Street. Turn right and then second right to join the towpath under Glasgow Road. Continue easily along the banks of the river to Balloch on the southern shores of Loch Lomond. Balloch Castle Country Park offers glorious views of the loch and, if time allows, is well worth a diversion. Camping, B&B and hotel accommodation can be found in Balloch and cruises can be arranged on the loch.

Turn left and continue straight ahead at the first roundabout to join the A82 at the second. Turn right and follow this north with stunning views across the loch.

Loch Lomond   **10.5 miles/62.9 miles**   **(675.7 miles)**

Loch Lomond is the largest lake in Britain and is famous for its steam cruises from Balloch. Surrounded by high mountains the area is absolutely stunning.

The route along the western shore of the loch is 25 miles long and at the end of a hard day will seem all of that. Heart can be taken from the splendid setting beneath the shade of the peaks to the west rising to over 2500ft and the views across the mirrored waters to the peaks of Beinn Lomond (3192ft), Beinn Uird (1957ft) and Beinn Bhreac (1922ft) glowing in the setting sun. The shoreline has an abundance of viewpoints, each promising better than the last, and the experience is completed by overhanging beech and birch trees and the multitude of plants and flowers clinging to the rocky banks by the roadside. A youth hostel is passed at Inverbeg about two-thirds of the way along the loch. Campers will have to wait to reach Ardlui, situated at the northernmost tip of the loch, for a much needed rest.

Ardlui   **23.2 miles/86.1 miles**   **(698.9 miles)**

Camping: on A82, caravan only ¹/₄m N on right of A82; Hotel.
Rail Station, Summer Ferry to the east bank of the loch.
Ardlui has limited facilities but it has all that matters after a hard day in the saddle.

Wild camping on the shores of Loch Lomond

DAY 11: ARDLUI to SPEAN BRIDGE

Total Distance: 67.6 miles
Cycling Time: 5 hours 40 minutes

If the weather is favourable this will be one of the most memorable day's cycle touring one could hope for. It contains all the scenic diversity that typifies the west coast of Scotland. The route begins along the narrow Glen Falloch and Strath Fillan, overhung with beech and crowded by the surrounding peaks. The inhospitable wilderness of Rannoch Moor offers a complete contrast and has the cyclist seeking the security of Glen Coe with the mountain scenery as dramatic as anywhere in Scotland. The coastal road now leads from Glen Coe to the town of Fort William along the shores of Loch Linnhe with views across Strathclyde to the Irish Sea. The day finishes beneath the slopes of Britain's highest mountain rising a full 4406ft above sea level. It is by no means an easy day's cycling, especially after the arduous ride of the previous day, but the rewards offered by

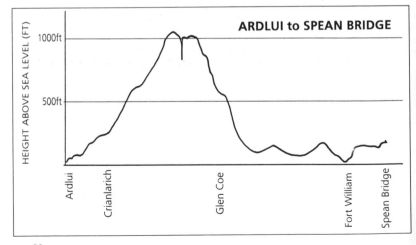

the scenery of this part of the country will certainly help to speed progress during these final few days of the tour.

| **Ardlui** | **0 miles** | **(698.9 miles)** |

From Ardlui the road continues between steep walls of rock that form Glen Falloch. Pass the Falls of Falloch and continue to Crianlarich situated at the junction of Glen Dochart, Glen Falloch and Strath Fillan (7.9 miles). There is a youth hostel here, a rail station, a hotel and a mountain rescue post but very little else.

Pass under the single track line to turn left, passing beneath the track once more before continuing on the A82 along Strath Fillan. The glen is wider here and allows more time to take in the views of the surrounding hills.

A brief climb leads to Tyndrum which has a rail station, tourist information, hotel, campsite and general provision stores.

The road continues north with the peak of Bienn Dorain (3524ft) dominating the skyline ahead. Climb sharply at first and then more easily before beginning the descent into Auch Gleann and the Bridge of Orchy. Easier ground now follows to the picturesque shores of Loch Tulla before climbing steeply once more to the Black Mount and onto the plateau of Rannoch Moor.

Rannoch Moor

The moor was shaped by the debris formed by the glacial sculpting of Glen Coe. The area is today one of the largest moorland wildernesses in the country, covering over 60 square miles of peat bogs, lochs, rivers and marshland. The high peaks that dominate the scene merely serve to emphasise the isolation and even during fine weather the moor appears quite inhospitable.

The road maintains a continuous climb into Glen Coe which tests even the strongest of legs. The entrance to Glen Coe is guarded by the peaks of Beinn a'Chrulaiste and Buachaille Etive Mor, providing the visitor with an uncomfortable welcome. The glen often channels a westerly wind which makes the cycling that much more of a challenge but the scenery more than compensates. A final welcome descent is made off the moor and the road enters Glen Coe.

Glen Coe
(732.9 miles)   **34 miles**

Probably the most famous of all the Scottish glens for its awe-inspiring mountain scenery and its history of murder and betrayal. It was here in 1692 that the MacDonald Clan were brutally murdered in their beds. The homesteads of the slaughtered clansmen are marked on the hillsides as a reminder of this despicable deed.

The mountain scenery of the area is quite unforgettable with the towering peaks of Buachaille Etive Mor, Bidean Nam Bian, Aonach and Eagach rising to the high corries and hanging valleys draped with cascading pearls of water. The area becomes very crowded during peak times and special care is advised as the majority of motorists will have one eye on the road and one on the mountains. Much of the area is now managed by the National Trust for Scotland. At the head of the glen by the banks of Loch Leven lies the village of Glencoe.

Continue along the A82 to the bridge at the head of the loch. Here the scenery suddenly changes and one is transported from classic upland mountain into a rugged, coastal setting. The road now follows the headland around the base of the peaks of Beinn an Aonch Mhoir and Beinn na Gucaig to the town of Fort William.

Fort William   **25.5 miles/59.5 miles**   **(758.4 miles)**

Campsite: 2¹/₂m N off A82, 2m N off A830; B&B, Hotels.

Tourist Information, Rail Station, Hospital, Post Office, Bank, Library, Cycle Shop, Shops.

Fort William lies at the head of Loch Linnhe and at the foot of Benn Nevis (4406ft), the highest mountain in Great Britain. The town serves as a popular base for climbers in the area in both summer and winter and the rail journey to Mallaig is one of the most scenic in the country. The fort from which the town derives its name was dismantled in the 19th century. The Caledonian Canal was built by Brunel to link the North Sea with the Irish Sea and culminates outside Fort William in a series of eight locks known as Neptune's Staircase. The canal drops a height of 90ft in 2 miles before joining the Irish Sea at the junction of Loch Linnhe and Loch Eil.

The A82 leads out of Fort William to pass the distillery and the golf course. The whale-backed peak of Ben Nevis is clearly visible with the Allt a Mhuilinn leading up into the dark recesses of the north face cliffs. The mountain holds snow for most of the summer months and an ascent at any time of the year should not be treated lightly.

The road continues easily through the Leanachan Forest to reach Spean Bridge.

Spean Bridge
8.1 miles/67.6 miles (766.5 miles)
The area has an abundance of campsites, a hotel and a small shop and makes an excellent location for an overnight stop. A memorial to the commandos that used the area as a training ground during the Second World War stands at the junction of the glens.

DAY 12: SPEAN BRIDGE to DINGWALL

Total Distance: **63.3 miles**
Cycling Time: **4 hours 25 minutes**

After the rigours of the previous day's ride, the route continues along a more leisurely course with generally easy cycling for the full distance. The day's journey crosses the country along the line of the Great Glen, an ancient fault that almost splits the country in two, and traces the course of the Caledonian Canal. The majority of the journey follows the shores of some of Scotland's great lochs.

The day begins along the shores of Loch Lochy before crossing to the west bank of Loch Oich and then continuing by the famous Loch Ness. The only real climb of the day is then encountered to escape from the Great Glen to the Beauly Firth and finally on to Dingwall on the west coast. It is a significant day on the route to John O'Groats as it psychologically brings the finish line within striking distance. The day's ride enjoys some of Scotland's more pastoral scenery which is by no means disappointing.

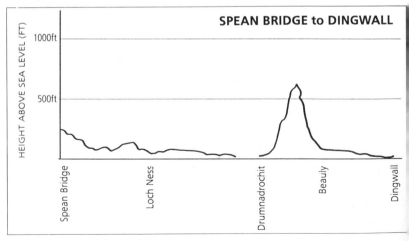

Spean Bridge　　　　**0 miles**　　　　　　**(766.5 miles)**

Leave Spean Bridge on the A82 to pass the memorial to the wartime commandos at the junction with the B8004. Climb briefly over a wooded hummock to descend below the steep hillside of Coire Ceirsle before joining the River Gloy on its descent to the banks of Loch Lochy. Peaks rise steeply all around from the depths of the mirrored loch waters, creating a truly memorable scene.

The road undulates easily beneath a canopy of greenery which all helps to maintain a steady pace. At the head of the loch a final descent leaves the Laggan Forest and crosses the Caledonian Canal.

Work on the canal was commenced by Telford in 1804 and took 18 years to complete. The purpose of the project was to utilise the natural fault across the country and forge a route from the Irish Sea to the North Sea, therefore avoiding the hazardous journey around the Scottish headland. The canal runs for 60 miles from Corpach to the Moray Firth, passing through 29 lochs including Loch Lochy, Loch Oich and Loch Ness. The first complete passage after the canal's completion was made in 1822. The canal is now used almost exclusively by pleasure craft.

Invergarry provides the opportunity for a rest stop at the head of Loch Oich, at the point where the River Garry drains into the basin. The hamlet acts as a delightful tourist centre for exploring the area and offers all forms of accommodation with easy access to the surrounding hills.

Continue along the west bank of Loch Oich before crossing the Caledonian Canal once more. The route to Fort Augustus picks a course through the glacial hillocks deposited at the head of the most famous of all Scottish lochs.

Loch Ness

The loch is 20 miles long and barely 1 mile wide but has a recorded depth of over 1000ft. The inky black waters resist all attempts to view the hidden depths, even with the most powerful modern underwater lighting systems. The fame of the loch hinges on an elusive monster that is claimed to inhabit the waters. Nothing conclusive has ever been found despite numerous scientific studies of the area.

Fort Augustus　　　　**22.1 miles**　　　　　　**(788.6 miles)**

Camping: $^{1}/_{2}$m S off A82.

Popular tourist centre. The name comes from William Augustus, Duke of Cumberland, who made the fort his quarters following success at the Battle of Culloden in 1746. The building was eventually donated to the Benedictine order who transformed it into an abbey. It is now a very successful school.

The road continues along the bank of the loch below Portclair Forest with a short detour to cross the River Moriston at Invermoriston. Creagnaneun Forest now hugs the steep slopes above Loch Ness.

The small headland at Strone stands guard over Urquhart Bay and is the site of Urquhart Castle. The castle dates from the 14th century and was the home of the chief of the clans from the 16th century until it was damaged during the Jacobite uprising of 1692. The castle is a favourite monster lookout point.

Drumnadrochit

The name means "Ridge of the Bridge" although it is little more than a collection of farmhouses. The town hosts two "Monster" exhibitions, both of which are well worth visiting.

The road now turns inland to cross the rivers Coiltie and Enrick at Drumnadrochit, which has a beautiful village green and village store providing welcome refreshments. Continue west on the A831 for about 1 mile to pass the village of Milton before taking a sharp turn right on the A833. The road is steep, narrow and twisting which provides a gruelling testpiece after

the morning's lakeside cruise. As the gradient increases to over 20% only the determined will remain in the saddle. The angle gradually relents to deliver the cyclist into an upland wilderness of mystic lochs and rolling hills. The occasional cattle grid and uniform shape of the tree plantations provide

the only clues to man's intrusion here. All too soon the descent begins, first steeply through Glen Convinth and then more gently along a series of shaded roller-coaster rides. The A833 joins the A862 which is taken left to cross the River Beauly. The A862 leads off immediately right into the small town of Beauly.

Beauly   **32.5 miles/54.6 miles**   **(821.1 miles)**

Camping: 2 sites up and downstream of the bridge.
The town was named in praise of the setting of a priory built by French monks in the 13th century but is probably better known today for the salmon fishing.

The road continues north across the sediments of the Beauly Firth to reach the Muir of Ord and on to Cononbridge to cross the Cromarty Firth. Continue straight over the roundabout to reach Dingwall.

Dingwall   **8.7 miles/63.3 miles**   **(829.8 miles)**

Camping: ¹/₂m E off Maryburgh Road; B&B, Hotels.
Tourist Information, Post Office, Bank, Cinema, Library, Cycle Shop, Shops.

Dingwall was named by Norse invaders that captured the town during the first century and literally means "A place of parliament". The town has always held a strategic value at the head of the Cromarty Firth and its location is no less important today as a holiday centre and an ideal base for exploring the Highlands. The town still fulfils a useful role as a market centre for the surrounding farming community.

The Town House Museum recounts the town's long history and has a special display dedicated to the memory of Hector McDonald for his distinguished military service. A monument stands in his honour on Mitchell Hill south of the town.

An alternative to the central section of the day's route is to take advantage of sections of the Forest Enterprise cycle route opened in 1992. The route follows the Caledonian Canal towpath from Fort William before utilising a number of forest tracks. The surface is generally good although some sections can be very muddy and only really suited for mountain bikes or lightly laden touring bikes. Access points are at Fort William, Spean Bridge and the Cherry Island car park 1 mile north of Fort Augustus. The track has good views across the lake and leads from Fort Augustus to Invermoriston on the Dalcataig Road. From Invermoriston a steep narrow tarmac road is climbed before a track can be picked up through the Creagnaneun Forest to arrive at the Loch Ness Youth Hostel. Total distance covered by this route is 11.6 miles and makes a pleasant change from the A82 if the weather is good.

For further details contact The Forest Enterprise at the address provided.

DAY 13: DINGWALL to HELMSDALE

Total Distance: **65.8 miles**
Cycling Time: **5 hours 35 minutes**

It is tempting to relax at this stage of the ride in the belief that John O'Groats is only a short ride up the coast. Geographically this may be correct as most of the route-finding has been completed but there is still over 120 miles to be covered to the journey's end. The main road leaves Dingwall along the banks of the Cromarty Firth before striking out north over the last plateau that bars northern progress. From here the route continues in a low lying plain with the mountains of Sutherland to the west. Some of the earliest examples of man's habitation of the British Isles can be found along this stretch of coastline with numerous cairns, standing stones and hill forts. More recently there are traces of early Christian chapels and medieval castles littering the rugged coastline. Bonar Bridge marks the beginning of the coast road and some very pleasant cycling. Helmsdale provides the overnight resting place that brings John O'Groats within striking distance.

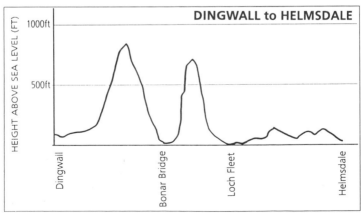

Dingwall   **0 miles**   **(829.8 miles)**

Leave Dingwall north on the A862 to cross the rail line and continue along the banks of Cromarty Firth. Pass under the railway bridge to continue at the water's edge with views ahead to the main A9 spanning the mouth of the estuary. Join the A9 at the bridge and continue with expanding views of the many sand bays that fringe the sparkling waters. The area has much evidence of the oil industry that thrives in the inhospitable waters of the North Sea and the Firth has established itself as a launch site for the many rigs that can be seen on the distant horizon.

Take the first turning left to pass under the rail line to reach the small town of Evanton. Continue straight through the town to reach the A836 which is taken left and commence climbing. The road strikes out north to cut across the headland that separates the Cromarty and Dornoch Firths, providing a convenient short-cut to Bonar Bridge. However the route doesn't give up without a fight and although there are no particularly steep sections the climb is long and steady. A short welcome descent crosses the River Averon before continuing into more open terrain to reach a small gravel car park on the Strath Rory River that marks the end of the climb. A strategically placed van supplies much needed refreshment!

A more undulating route

through a forested region now follows, before the descent begins in earnest. The views across the Dornoch Firth provide an exciting climax as the road arrives at a junction with the A9. Turn

left and continue easily along the estuary to cross at a headland to Bonar Bridge.

Bonar Bridge 27 miles (856.8 miles)

Campsite: 3m W on A836; B&B.
Tourist Information, Cafe, General Stores, Cycle Shop.
The bridge spans the channel that links the Kyle of Sutherland to the sea and was originally designed by Telford in 1812.

The remaining cycling for the day is very gentle and follows a leisurely course along beautiful country lanes that wouldn't seem out of place in central England were it not for the unique Scottish views that appear through the lush canopy of beech, birch, oak and alder.

First continue along the estuary before turning north through small hamlets and villages to arrive at The Mound by the junction with the A39 just beyond Loch Fleet. Continue easily along the A9 to the coast at Golspie.

The coastal scenery in this part of Scotland is every bit as exciting as the rugged west coast and is far more varied. Rocky headlands constantly divert the road course from its north-easterly progress and sandy bays tempt the traveller to linger a while before continuing the journey.

The small town of Brora lies nestled beneath a rocky inlet carved by the River Brora as it drains the high peaks to the west. In contrast to the rugged cliffs the sheltered bay to the north of the town appears quite serene as its golden sands radiate the warmth of the setting sun.

101

Brora   **27.9 miles/54.9 miles**   **(884.7 miles)**

Two campsites, B&B, Hotel.
Cycle Shop.
The town is mainly a tourist centre for salmon fishing in the area. The main industry is the spinning of Shetland wool. The town is perfectly adequate for an overnight stop but in an effort to reduce the final day's mileage it may be worth persevering with the remaining 11 miles to Helmsdale.

Helmsdale   **10.9 miles/65.8 miles**   **(895.6 miles)**

Campsite, B&B.

Tourist Information, Rail Station, Hospital, Shops.
The River Helmsdale cuts a fierce channel through the hills that rise steeply from its banks and squeezes the town between Creag Bun - Ullidh and the rocky coastline. The town still reveals examples of a former wealth built up around the herring fishing industry. The herring have gone now but fishing is still the main industry with catches of whitebait and lobster being predominant. A local exhibition traces the history of the highlands and is worth a visit if time permits. The Duke of Sutherland chose the town as a showpiece and the streets were all renamed after his Scottish estates.

Unsettled weather may be encountered at any time. The secret is to be prepared

DAY 14: HELMSDALE to JOHN O'GROATS

Total Distance: **51 miles**
Cycling Time: **3 hours 45 minutes**

The concluding leg of the journey follows the north-east coast road out of the highlands and into the open moorlands characteristic of the Scottish north coast. The town of Wick offers all facilities to the traveller but other than that the route follows a lonely course. Taken in isolation the day would not be considered the most memorable of cycle tours, especially if the weather was less than perfect, which it very often is, but as a climax to a tour that has spanned the countryside of Great Britain it is a fitting finale. The final stretch from Wick to the north-eastern tip is as isolated as expected and lives up to all preconceptions that one may associate with this part of the journey. Emotions tend to be a mixture of jubilation and disappointment. Jubilation, obviously, because the trip has reached a successful conclusion and any rider completing the full distance can feel justly proud. On the other hand there is always the anticlimax that accompanies the completion of a project such as this. Maybe it's time to start planning the next trip? How about a route around the British coastline?

It is advisable to make an early start to allow for the mandatory "end of tour" celebrations and to sort out the tiresome task of arranging transportation home.

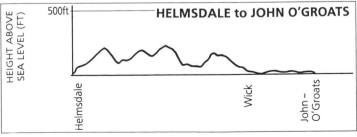

Helmsdale   **0 miles**   **(895.6 miles)**

As if to discourage any feelings of complacency that may accompany the last day, the route begins with a steep ascent from the town. Stunning views along the rugged coastline and out into the bleak waters of the North Sea are the rewards for the effort as the road winds along before descending once more. A series of steep descents with the inevitable reascents help to maintain interest until a final freewheel leads down into Berriedale. What had promised to be a well deserved refreshment stop from a distance turns out to be little more than a collection of houses and forces another few miles of short climbs from weary legs before the village of Dunbeath offers welcome sanctuary. The village has a campsite, a pier and, most importantly, a shop!

As the route continues it is noticeable that the ridges and peaks of the highlands have receded onto the western horizon and been replaced by more open grassland combed by the relentless winds that sweep this north-eastern headland. The road winds northward to pass a junction with the A895 at Latheron.

The solitude of the area appears to be enhanced by irregular scatterings of single cottages and small hamlets and the meandering drystone walls that criss-cross the area between the road and the coast. The coastline too appears more dramatic with steep cliffs and isolated stacks pounded by fierce waves driven by the strong North Sea swells. The small hamlet of Whaligoe is testament to the inhabitants' defiance of these elements where a flight of over 300 steps has been carved into the rock down to a tiny harbour beneath the cliffs.

The road levels once more

and by the time the village of Thrumster is reached the cycling has become quite straightforward.

Wick 34.9 miles (930.5 miles)

Campsite: ¹/₂m W on A882; B&B, Guest Houses, Hotels. Tourist Information, Rail Station, Airport, Hospital, Post Office, Bank, Cinema, Library, Shops.

Wick appears on the horizon like an oasis in the desert with promises of refreshments to satiate the weariest of travellers. The town is positioned at the head of Wick Bay, a natural harbour since ancient times. In fact the name is derived from the Norse meaning "Bay". The town's prosperity revolved around the herring fishing industry and today it serves as a market centre for the north-east with a reputation for hand-blown glass. A local airstrip services the northern Isles as well as providing a communication link to the southern mainland.

The departure from Wick marks the final milestone on a tour that has taken almost two weeks to complete. It is perhaps for this reason that there seems some reluctance to embark upon it. Hunger for success eventually prevails and the cycle is mounted for the final section.

The A9 leaves the town centre north to pass the twin ruins of

Sinclair and Girnigoe castles clinging precariously to the cliff tops. The castles were once the stronghold of the Earls of Caithness. The road turns right after about 3 miles at the junction with the B876 and once more seeks out the coastline across a harsh landscape of coarse tussock grassland. A short climb over Warth Hill leads to the final descent to the coast and the small village of John O'Groats.

John O'Groats   16.1 miles/51 miles   (946.6 miles)

Campsite: 1m W on A836, John O'Groats; B&B, Hotel.

This collection of pretty cottages has, in fact, no geographical significance. Duncansby Head is the true north-easterly point of the British Isles and Dunnet Head is the most northerly point. However neither location has much to offer the visitor and it is therefore John O'Groats that has become the established opposite to Lands End. The views from all three locations are spectacular across the galloping white horses to the islands of Stroma and Orkney. The name of the village is said to have been derived from Jan de Groot, a Dutchman who operated the ferries to the islands in the 15th century.

Congratulations!

The John O'Groats House Hotel and the end of a memorable trip

APPENDICES

1: LANDS END to JOHN O'GROATS RECORDS

Men

Bicycle	A. Wilkinson 1990 1 day 21 hours 2 minutes 18 seconds
Tricycle:	R. Dadswell 1992 2 days 5 hours 29 minutes 1 second
Tandem:	P. Swinden & W. Withers 1966 2 days 2 hours 14 minutes 25 seconds

Women

Bicycle:	P. Strong 1991 2 days 6 hours 49 minutes 45 seconds
Walking:	M. Barnish 12 days 3 hours 45 minutes
Hitch Hiking:	M. Clark & J. Benyon 1987 17 hours 8 minutes
Running:	D. Ritchie 1989 10 days 15 hours 27 minutes

2: ADDITIONAL INFORMATION

Lands End to John O'Groats Association
   2 Coastguard Cottages,
   Penberth, St Buryan, Penzance, Cornwall TR19 6HJ

Cyclists' Touring Club
   Cotterell House, 69 Meadrow, Godalming, Surrey GU7 3HS

Sustrans Scotland
   53 Cochrane Street, Glasgow G1 1HL

Youth Hostel Association
   Trevelyan House, 8 St Stephen's Hill, St Albans AL1 2DY

Scottish Youth Hostel Association
   7 Glebe Crescent, Stirling FK8 2JA

Bike Events may be contacted on 01225 310859 for information
   regarding organised trips from Lands End to John O'Groats.

British Tourist Authority & English Tourist Board
   Thames Tower, Blacks Road, Hammersmith, London W6 9EL

Scottish Tourist Board
   23 Ravelston Terrace, Edinburgh EH4 3EU

West Country Tourist Board
   37 Southernhay East, Exeter, Devon EX1 1QS

North West Tourist Board
   The Last Drop Village, Bromley Cross, Bolton, Lancashire BL7
   9PZ

Lancashire Cycle Way
   Details available free from PO Box 78, Lancashire County
   Council, County Hall, Preston PR1 8XJ

Cumbria Tourist Board
   Ashleigh, Holly Road, Windermere LA23 2AQ

Cumbrian Cycle Way
   Leaflet available price £1.50 plus p+p. Cumbrian County
   Council, County Planning Dept, County Offices, Kendal,
   Cumbria LA9 4RU.
   Accommodation guide for the above route available from
   Hilary Claxton, The Old Court House, High Street, Kirkby
   Stephen, Cumbria (£1 + SAE)

   The Cumbria Cycle Way by Walker & Jarvis. Cicerone Press,
   2 Police Square, Milnthorpe, Cumbria LA7 7PY

Great Glen Cycle Route
   Forest Enterprise North Scotland,
   Inverness District, Smithton, Inverness IV1 2NL

Glasgow - Loch Lomond - Killin Cycleway
Details free from Loch Lomond, Stirling and Trossachs Tourist
   Board, 41 Dumbarton Road, Stirling FK8 2QQ

CICERONE GUIDES

Cicerone publish a wide range of reliable guides to walking and climbing abroad

FRANCE, BELGIUM & LUXEMBOURG
CHAMONIX MONT BLANC - A Walking Guide
THE CORSICAN HIGH LEVEL ROUTE: GR20
FRENCH ROCK
THE PYRENEAN TRAIL: GR10
THE RLS (Stevenson) TRAIL
ROCK CLIMBS IN BELGIUM & LUXEMBOURG
ROCK CLIMBS IN THE VERDON
TOUR OF MONT BLANC
TOUR OF THE OISANS: GR54
TOUR OF THE QUEYRAS
WALKING THE FRENCH ALPS: GR5
WALKING THE FRENCH GORGES (Provence)
WALKS IN VOLCANO COUNTRY (Auvergne)
THE WAY OF ST JAMES: GR65

FRANCE / SPAIN
WALKS AND CLIMBS IN THE PYRENEES
ROCK CLIMBS IN THE PYRENEES

SPAIN & PORTUGAL
ANDALUSIAN ROCK CLIMBS
BIRDWATCHING IN MALLORCA
COSTA BLANCA CLIMBS
MOUNTAIN WALKS ON THE COSTA BLANCA
WALKING IN MALLORCA
WALKS & CLIMBS IN THE PICOS DE EUROPA
THE WAY OF ST JAMES: SPAIN
WALKING IN THE ALGARVE

FRANCE / SWITZERLAND
CHAMONIX TO ZERMATT The Walker's Haute Route
THE JURA - Walking the High Route and Winter Ski
    Traverses

SWITZERLAND
THE ALPINE PASS ROUTE
THE BERNESE ALPS
CENTRAL SWITZERLAND
THE GRAND TOUR OF MONTE ROSA (inc Italy)
WALKS IN THE ENGADINE
WALKING IN TICINO
THE VALAIS - A Walking Guide

GERMANY / AUSTRIA / EASTERN EUROPE
HUT-TO-HUT IN THE STUBAI ALPS
THE HIGH TATRAS
THE KALKALPEN TRAVERSE
KING LUDWIG WAY
KLETTERSTEIG - Scrambles
MOUNTAIN WALKING IN AUSTRIA
WALKING IN THE BLACK FOREST
WALKING IN THE HARZ MOUNTAINS
WALKING IN THE SALZKAMMERGUT

ITALY & SLOVENIA
ALTA VIA - High Level Walks in the Dolomites
CLASSIC CLIMBS IN THE DOLOMITES
THE GRAND TOUR OF MONTE ROSA inc Switzerland))
ITALIAN ROCK - Rock Climbs in Northern Italy
VIA FERRATA - Scrambles in the Dolomites
WALKING IN THE DOLOMITES
WALKS IN THE JULIAN ALPS

MEDITERRANEAN COUNTRIES
THE ATLAS MOUNTAINS
CRETE: Off the beaten track
THE MOUNTAINS OF GREECE
THE MOUNTAINS OF TURKEY
TREKS & CLIMBS IN WADI RUM, JORDAN
THE ALA DAG - Climbs & Treks (Turkey)

OTHER COUNTRIES
ADVENTURE TREKS - W. N. AMERICA
ANNAPURNA TREKKERS GUIDE
CLASSIC TRAMPS IN NEW ZEALAND
MOUNTAIN WALKING IN AFRICA 1: KENYA
ROCK CLIMBS IN HONG KONG
TREKKING IN THE CAUCASUS
TREKKING IN NEPAL
TREKKING - WESTERN NORTH AMERICA

GENERAL OUTDOOR BOOKS
THE ADVENTURE ALTERNATIVE
FAMILY CAMPING
FIRST AID FOR HILLWALKERS
THE HILL WALKERS MANUAL
LIMESTONE -100 BEST CLIMBS IN BRITAIN
MOUNTAIN WEATHER
MOUNTAINEERING LITERATURE
MODERN ALPINE CLIMBING
MODERN SNOW & ICE TECHNIQUES
ROPE TECHNIQUES IN MOUNTAINEERING

CANOEING
CANOEIST'S GUIDE TO THE NORTH EAST
SNOWDONIA WILD WATER, SEA & SURF
WILDWATER CANOEING

CARTOON BOOKS
ON FOOT & FINGER
ON MORE FEET & FINGERS
LAUGHS ALONG THE PENNINE WAY
THE WALKERS

*Also a full range of guidebooks
to walking, scrambling, ice-climbing,
rock climbing, and other adventurous
pursuits in Britain and abroad*

*Other guides are constantly being added to the Cicerone List.
Available from bookshops, outdoor equipment shops or direct (send for price list)
from CICERONE, 2 POLICE SQUARE, MILNTHORPE, CUMBRIA, LA7 7PY*

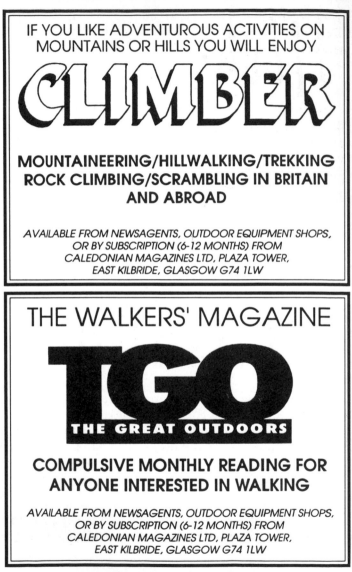
Printed by CARNMOR PRINT & DESIGN
95-97 LONDON ROAD, PRESTON, LANCASHIRE, UK.